CONTENTS

Acknowledgements

This is the final report of a project that would not have been possible without generous support from Edexcel, the Learning and Skills Council (LSC), the National Institute for Adult and Continuing Education (NIACE) and Ufl Ltd.

A series of policy seminars that informed this project and report were held during 2006, with useful contributions from Chris Barnham (Department for Education and Skills), Leon Feinstein (Institute of Education), Jon Gamble and Rob Wye (Learning and Skills Council), Alissa Goodman (Institute for Fiscal Studies), Francis Green (University of Kent), Ann Hodgson, Ken Spours and Lorna Unwin (Institute of Education), Deirdre Macleod (Policyworks) and Alan Wells (Basic Skills Agency).

The project has benefited from a number of helpful discussions, and from comments on a first draft of the report. Contributors included Steve Besley (Edexcel), David Coats (The Work Foundation), Mark Corney, Julie Nugent (Learning and Skills Council), Ian Pryce (Bedford College), David Sherlock (Adult Learning Inspectorate), Sarah-Jane Smalley (Ufi), Alastair Thomson and Alan Tuckett (NIACE) and John West (University of Leicester). Particular thanks go to Mick Fletcher and Geoff Stanton for their support throughout the project.

Thanks are also due to my ippr colleagues, including John Cannings, Adam Marshall, Max Nathan, Nick Pearce, Howard Reed and, particularly, Richard Brooks, for their valuable input and advice.

Many thanks go to all of the above, to those who participated in the seminars and to the many others who helped with the research. However, the views expressed in this report are solely those of the author.

LEARNING FOR LIFE

A NEW FRAMEWORK FOR ADULT SKILLS

SIMONE DELORENZI

ippr

The Institute for Public Policy Research is the UK's leading progressive think tank, producing cutting-edge research and innovative policy ideas for a just, democratic and sustainable world. Since 1988, we have been at the forefront of progressive debate and policymaking in the UK. Through our independent research and analysis we define new agendas for change and provide practical solutions to challenges across the full range of public policy issues. With offices in both London and Newcastle, we ensure our outlook is as broad-based as possible, while our international team and climate change programme extend our partnerships and influence beyond the UK, giving us a truly world-class reputation for high quality research.

For further information you can contact ippr's external affairs department on info@ippr.org, you can view our website at www.ippr.org and you can buy our books from Central Books on 0845 458 9910 or email ippr@centralbooks.com.

Our trustees

© IPPR 2007

About the author

Simone Delorenzi is a research fellow at the Institute for Public Policy Research (ippr), specialising in education. Her publications at ippr include *Choosing to Learn: Improving participation after compulsory education* (with Peter Robinson, 2005) and *Maintaining Momentum: Promoting social mobility and life chances from early years to adulthood* (co-edited with Jodie Reed and Peter Robinson, 2005).

Executive summary

New Labour made an early commitment to 'lifelong learning', and has significantly increased the resources allocated to further education. Despite this, adult learners have less choice over what they are allowed to study, get less financial support, and are often taught by less stable, lower paid staff than their peers in universities. Those who dropped out of school early on with few or no qualifications are likely to find it even more difficult to engage in education in later life, losing out on the benefits that learning can bring them in terms of employment and social integration. A new framework needs to be devised in order to make it easier for them to return to learning and to gain the most from it.

A second chance at education and training

Participation in adult learning is relatively high in England, compared with other industrialised countries. However, those who are most disadvantaged by their initial education, employment and income are the least likely to be involved in learning. Relatively few young people stay on in education after 16 compared to other countries, and socio-economic inequalities tend to be wider. The main aim of adult learning should be to help those who missed out on education the first time round.

The objectives of adult learning

We should start with the benefits that adult learning can bring to individuals. Acquiring skills and qualifications as an adult can lead to better outcomes in the labour market, particularly for disadvantaged groups. Although wage premiums to qualifications gained as adults remain low, the chances of being in employment rise significantly with each additional qualification level. Specific indicators, such as the likelihood of giving up smoking or doing more exercise, also show that adult learning can have a wider impact on the lives of individuals, families and communities than direct economic benefits alone.

Government policy on the one hand, and the latest Leitch Review of Skills (Leitch 2006) on the other, put employers, rather than individuals, in the driving seat through initiatives such as Train to Gain and the Sector Skills Councils.

Adult learning, skills and qualifications

The Government's adult learning policy is increasingly focused on two

Public Service Agreement (PSA) targets – to increase the number of people with basic skills, and to increase the number with level 2 qualifications (equivalent to five GCSEs at grades A* to C). These targets have helped focus attention on the 6.7 million people of working age with low education attainment. But they have also led to increasingly narrow provision, focused disproportionately on those with the 'least distance to travel', and bypassing those with the greatest need for skills.

The two qualifications attached to the targets – basic skills and National Vocational Qualifications (NVQs) – are often used as a way of certifying existing skills rather than helping to acquire new ones. One of the characteristics of such programmes has been to try to make it easy for people to acquire qualifications by removing the requirement to learn anything new. Not only does this bring little benefit to candidates – it also devalues the qualifications. The wage premiums attached to these qualifications are minimal.

Funding, fees and financial support

The government policy on fees and financial support for learners is also increasingly geared towards the two PSA targets. Those without basic skills or a level 2 qualification are entitled to free tuition to study for a first full qualification at these levels – as do those without a level 3 (A-level equivalent) up to the age of 25. Increasingly, adults wanting to access other types of provision have to pay for them. In the past, fee remissions and fee subsidies have often benefited learners indiscriminately, and there is a strong case for raising fees if this allows better targeting of those who need more support.

However, the entitlements only give access to specific types of provision – namely, a first full qualification at level 2 or 3 – and this means that some beneficiaries are unable to access the courses that would suit them most. People are not allowed to access a level 1 or partial level 2 qualification, for example.

Additionally, financial support has not been adapted to the needs of adult learners who have to pay increasing fees. Unlike higher education students, who are able to defer payment of their tuition fees with income-contingent loans at zero interest rates, those in further education have to pay up front or start repaying their Career Development Loans straight after their study, and at commercial interest rates.

The institutional framework

The Learning and Skills Council (LSC) was created in 2001 as a body with strong responsibilities to plan for the provision and structure of further education. Since then, the Government has shifted the emphasis of the body towards the introduction of market mechanisms, such as choice, specialisation and competition.

However, adult learning most resembles a mixed economy, where providers are heavily influenced by LSC funding and targets, and are only really in competition to gain LSC funding. This is quite different from operating in a real market. The result has been increasing regulation, as the Government wants to ensure that its resources are used in its favoured way, and increasing instability, as learning providers constantly have to adapt to changes in national priorities and initiatives. Often, reforms introduced in the name of the 'market' have simply led to a different form of centralised planning, and learning providers have seen their autonomy increasingly reduced.

The recommendation by the Leitch Review to fund providers only after they have secured enrolments and achievements would introduce yet another element of instability into the system.

Much energy and many resources have been spent in trying to create a market for adult learning, and in giving more powers to employers to plan for provision in their sector, through the Sector Skills Councils (as well as giving them free training). This approach should be reversed, starting with the learner and empowering learning providers to respond to their demand.

Key recommendations

Recommendation 1: Articulate a new rationale for adult learning

- **Emphasise the individual objectives of adult learning** A better balance needs to be achieved between the different objectives for adult learning. Improvements in labour market outcomes for individuals, together with other benefits of learning, such as better health or social integration, should be seen as the conditions for improving macro-economic and fiscal outcomes. The new framework for adult learning needs to start with the needs of individuals rather than the needs of employer bodies.

- **Focus on priority groups** Government subsidy for adult learning needs to focus on priority groups – those with no or low qualifications, the unemployed, and specific categories of people with low rates of economic activity such as mothers returning to work. It should ensure that members of these groups can easily access an appropriate range of learning options. For everyone else, the Government's responsibility should be to make sure that affordable, quality provision (for which learners will have to pay some or most of the cost) is available.

Recommendation 2: Put learners and learning at the centre of the system

- **Prioritise learner choice** Individual learners should be allowed to choose the type of provision that they want to access. They should be able to focus not just on obtaining qualifications, but also on learning and acquiring new skills. They should be able to decide whether or not to study towards a qualification and, if they do want to, to choose the type of qualification. Not all courses should be expected to lead towards costly, externally accredited qualifications.

We should also reconsider whether colleges should be allowed to develop their own awards, with a degree of external validation potentially offered by the Open College Network or the Qualifications and Credit Framework.

- **Ensure new flexible entitlement for those without a level 2 qualification**
  Everyone without a level 2 qualification should be allowed free access to the provision of their choice up to level 2, including at entry level, level 1, and a partial level 2 (or 3, for those who are able to jump a level). Provision under this entitlement would not have to lead to an externally accredited qualification, but would be offered in addition to the existing entitlement to a first full level 2 qualification, so that the option to take a qualification would ultimately remain.

  This new entitlement would guarantee free tuition for the notional equivalent in guided learning hours of a two-year full-time course at level 2. This course could be taken flexibly over a period of time, either through intensive one-year courses or for a few hours a week over several years.

- **Run pilots for a modified Train to Gain and the new flexible entitlement**
  In line with the focus of the new framework on learners rather than employers, the Train to Gain programme should either be modified or give way to the new flexible entitlement. Employers should not expect to have their training paid for them by the state. Parallel pilots could evaluate the introduction of the new flexible entitlement in comparison with Train to Gain.

- **Provide general education for adults** People who come back to learning later in their lives should have the same rights to access general education as younger people do, and the current restrictions related to financial support should be lifted. Courses should be designed to provide general education for adults, including at level 2, as an alternative to the almost exclusively vocational qualifications currently on offer.

- **Strengthen information, advice and guidance** Choice and flexible entitlements should be supported with an improved system for information, advice and guidance. In-depth guidance on careers and learning opportunities should be easily accessible, both by telephone and face to face. While individuals should be able to access advice from a variety of sources, the current national systems need to be rationalised, with learndirect acting as the sole national public advice agency for all study levels.

Recommendation 3: Support learner choice

- **Provide flexible financial support** Discretionary funding, as currently provided through the discretionary fee remissions of colleges and Learner Support Funds, is the method of choice for supporting learners with indirect and one-off costs. The main criteria for distributing these funds should be based on student needs and income, rather than type of qualification pursued. Those studying at level 2 and below might also be offered some support towards living costs, alongside local grant systems.

- **Provide income-contingent loans** Adults taking level 3 or 4 courses in the learning and skills sector should be given access to income-contingent loans on the same basis as higher education (HE) students. The interest subsidy available to HE students should be extended to further education (FE) students – at least until a better system is devised for both groups. The Government should reconsider this issue when it reviews the funding arrangements for universities in 2009.

- **Encourage unemployed people to learn** The Government's employment policy has been based around the principle of 'work first', rather than encouraging the unemployed to learn. We need to reconsider whether practical arrangements can be made to improve access to learning for people in receipt of Jobseeker's Allowance while maintaining job search requirements. The 16-hour rule for study should be scrapped. Once someone has found a job, better coordination between the LSC and Jobcentre Plus should make it easier for them to finish a course that they started while unemployed, by studying in their own time. Jobcentre Plus learning provision responsibilities should be transferred to the LSC.

Recommendation 4: Enable learning providers and local government to respond to local demand

- **Ensure more devolution to learning providers** Like universities, further education colleges should be able to play a strategic role, defining their own mission and direction. Three-year plans should become the norm, to ensure better stability and long-term planning.

- **Ensure more devolution to local government** Local authorities and, where they exist, city regions, are best placed to identify the needs of their specific communities. They can also be held democratically accountable for the way local provision responds to these needs. As a result, local government should be the learning providers' main interlocutor in ascertaining demand for learning and ways to respond to it. The funding body should be required to spend the budget for any given area according to the agreements reached with local government and learning providers ('dual key' arrangements).

- **Slim down the Learning and Skills Council structure** The national office of the LSC should play the role of a funding body similar to the one that the Higher Education Funding Council of England (HEFCE) plays for higher education. Its main tasks would be to allocate resources to local areas on the basis of need, to agree learning providers' plans with the local government, and to monitor their spending. The Local Partnership Teams should be made co-terminous with local authorities or city regions. Their role should be limited to representing the national office at the local level. The regional offices would also have a much smaller role than they do at present, acting as a forum to facilitate coordination between adjacent local entities.

- **Abolish state subsidies to Sector Skills Councils** Sector Skills Councils should not add another layer of planning to the one already exercised by the LSC. The state should stop subsidising them, and the saved resources redirected towards funding of the new flexible entitlement and financial support for students. If employers feel that a skills council for their sector would be truly valuable, then it should be funded by an employer levy. Regional Development Agencies should have their role relating to skills limited to pulling together information from their local authorities and city regions.

Taken together, all these measures would go some way towards creating a leaner and less expensive structure, with individuals in the driving seat, making their own choices on the basis of information from employers and learning providers.

Introduction

The idea that we should all learn throughout our lives has become a common proposition. Changes in technology, legal requirements, career progression and the desire to explore new territory can all lead to a return to the classroom, whether in the form of a short session at work or a series of lectures in a large auditorium. In England, and thus in this report, the term 'adult learning' is used to encompass all education and training activities undertaken by adults over the age of 19 for professional or personal reasons. It excludes higher education, but includes general, vocational and enterprise training.

Because of its many diverse forms, adult learning is a difficult concept to grasp. This partly explains why it rarely makes the headlines and is seldom the subject of heated political debates. Also, few politicians and commentators have a direct experience of publicly funded further education, which is provided mainly in colleges and local community settings, as opposed to schools or universities. Further education is more likely to be attended by members of disadvantaged groups who have often left initial education at 16 and rarely get a chance to train at work. It is as a provider of 'second chances' that adult learning has a most significant role to play.

The notion of learning as a second chance is also what distinguishes adult education from provision for young people, even though the two forms may be very similar, targeting the same groups at different stages in their lives, and often taking place in the same institutions within the further education sector. An earlier report, *Choosing to Learn* (Delorenzi and Robinson 2005), explored the challenges related to improving participation for 16- to 19-year-olds, and showed the necessity of making the transition as smooth as possible. However, the political framework, funding and financial arrangements are significantly different for these two age groups, justifying the need to examine them separately.

Higher education (HE) also operates under a very different system, and is therefore not explored here, although useful parallels can be drawn between HE and adult learning.

Despite its low profile, adult learning has been in a state of almost constant revolution for some time. Over the past 15 years, colleges have been freed from local government control and have become expected to operate within a market. They have been asked to widen their offer in order to attract ever more people, and then to focus only on priority groups. Several new qualifications have been created, and teacher requirements have been toughened. Funding experienced a significant increase at the beginning of the millennium, but has generally been inadequate.

Many of the changes in adult learning have been triggered by external factors, such as the other priorities of the education budget, the demands of public service reform, and expressions of dissatisfaction with the overall education system voiced by the business sector.

About this report

The purpose of this report is to set out a clear, autonomous rationale for adult learning, and to inform the development of a new framework for publicly subsidised provision in England. It seeks to understand why the Government should become involved in adult learning, and what its main objectives should be. It seeks to identify the different groups that benefit from public provision and that should thus be able to choose which types of courses and training they can access. Finally, it explores the ways in which existing funding and institutional mechanisms can sometimes prevent people from getting appropriate provision.

Chapter 1 provides a brief overview of the current state of adult learning in England in comparison with other countries, and explores how it has evolved over time. Chapter 2 analyses the main rationales for adult learning – particularly within the skills debate. It evaluates how the system currently meets the Government's main objectives, and suggests a few principles for the new adult learning framework.

The following three chapters explore the evidence relating to the main policies adopted in three areas of adult learning, and make recommendations. First, Chapter 3 examines different forms of provision, and seeks to understand whether the main benefits of adult learning are derived from achieving qualifications, acquiring skills or being involved in the learning process. Then, Chapter 4 measures the impact of recent changes in funding and examines the extent to which the different forms of financial support benefit learners, asking how resources should be distributed in order to help those who need them most.

Finally, Chapter 5 focuses on institutions in the adult learning sector and the main funding and planning body of the sector – the Learning and Skills Council. It assesses the likely impact of ongoing reforms on the two top requirements: quality of provision and system efficiency.

The report is rounded off with a conclusion and a series of recommendations, which draw together policy recommendations and proposed directions for future research.

1. Policy context and key trends

In the past few years, the Labour government's early commitment to an extensive vision of lifelong learning has faded significantly. Provision of further education for adults is subject to financial pressure because of higher political priorities in schools and higher education, and is increasingly focused on supplying skills to the economy.

At the same time, the current picture for adult learning in England is a contradictory one. Participation is relatively high compared to other countries, but educational and socio-economic inequalities place a burden on the adult education and training system to reduce what is referred to as a 'skills gap' both between levels in England and those in other countries, and within the English economy itself.

From 'lifelong learning' to 'skills for the economy'

Since Tony Blair became leader of the Labour Party in 1994, the party has maintained three objectives of learning (Chitty 2004): economic productivity, personal fulfilment, and social cohesion. However, each of these priorities has been given various emphases at different times, and today, economic imperatives clearly supersede any other concerns. Labour has tried different approaches to adult learning policy throughout its years in government, including stimulating demand and widening participation, carrying out institutional reform of the education and training system, and drawing up a skills policy increasingly targeted at employers.

Box 1.1 provides a summary of learning and skills policy milestones since 1992.

Box 1.1: Learning and skills policy – milestones since 1992	
1992	Further and Higher Education Act. Creation of the Further Education Funding Council (FEFC) and legislation to free FE colleges from local authority control.
1997	New Deal for Young People for unemployed young people (including a full-time education option centred on NVQ 2), later followed by New Deal for 25+ and New Deal for 50+.
1998	*The Learning Age* (DfEE 1998). Expansive vision of 'lifelong learning'. Individual Learning Accounts (ILAs) and UfI Ltd, based on a concept of 'University for Industry'.
1999	*Learning to Succeed* (DfEE 1999) – Learning and Skills Council (LSC) to replace the FEFC and Training and Enterprise Councils (TECs), with additional planning function.
1999	Adult Learning Inspectorate (ALI) replaces Training Standards Inspectorate.
2000	National Skills Task Force Final Report (DfEE 2000)

cont. next page

2001	*Skills for Life* (DfEE 2001) – Entitlement to free basic skills (literacy and numeracy) tuition.
	Replacement of National Training Organisations (NTOs) with the Skills for Business Network, comprising Sector Skills Councils (SSC) and the Sector Skills Development Agency (SSDA).
	Cabinet Office Workforce Development Project: *In Demand: Adult skills in the 21st century* (Performance and Innovation Unit 2001).
2002	*Success for All* (DfES 2002) – Strategic Area Reviews, teacher and lecturer qualifications.
	Launch of Employer Training Pilots.
	Significant increase in funding.
2003	Launch of *21st Century Skills* (DfES/DTI/DWP/HMT 2003) – a joint skills strategy.
	Level 2 entitlement, Adult Learning Grant (ALG), budget for personal, community and development learning (PCDL) frozen, and colleges required to raise higher fees on non-priority courses.
2004	*Five-year Strategy for Children and Learners* (DfES 2004)
2005	*Skills Strategy: Getting on in business, getting on in work* (Skills White Paper, DfES/DTI/HMT/DWP 2005) – Skills Academies, Union Learning Academy and Next Step consultation.
	Foster Review of Further Education Final Report (Foster 2005)
	Skills in the UK – Leitch Review of Skills interim report (Leitch 2005)
2006	*Further Education: Raising skills, improving life chances* (Further Education White Paper, DfES 2006b) – FE colleges to focus on employability mission, level 3 entitlement (up to age 25), new learning accounts, Foundation Learning Tier
	Prosperity for All in the Global Economy – Leitch Review of Skills final report (Leitch 2006)

What we are witnessing is a move from a learner- and provider-led system to an employer-led system. Institutional reform, aimed at reorganising the provider base, has been present throughout Labour's years in office. But having started with a strongly planned approach, efforts are now focusing on turning the rhetoric of creating a genuine market for adult learning into reality.

These changing rationales have had a direct impact on public funding for adult learning, which has also been influenced by the wider context of the overall education budget. The rate of growth in overall education spending averaged 6.6 per cent a year in real terms between 1999/2000 and 2005/06 – much higher than the underlying rate of growth in the economy. It is now decelerating significantly, with an average of 2.6 per cent per year in real terms planned for 2006/07 and 2007/08.

Further spending will be defined through the 2007 Comprehensive Spending Review, but growth is likely to be slower than it was in the past, due to strong pressures in other areas of public spending (Goodman and Sibieta 2006).

The Government has already set clear priorities for education, emphasising early years, schools, 16- to 19-year-olds and higher education. What is left for adult learning is increasingly tied to the two PSA targets: improvements in basic skills, and achievement of level 2 qualifications (equivalent to five

GCSEs at grades A* to C) (DfES 2006a). As a result, non-priority areas of adult learning have been squeezed, and are likely to be squeezed even further.

Figure 1.1 gives an indication of how this has translated into funding through the Learning and Skills Council, since 2001. The four categories at the top cannot easily be distinguished by age. Learner support and development has grown significantly, but most of the recent growth has been driven by the new Education Maintenance Allowances for 16- to 19-year-olds. Capital grants and funding for learners with learning disabilities and/or difficulties have expanded regularly and significantly. After an initial increase, the funding for work-based learning (about one quarter of which goes to adults) has remained roughly constant.

The main beneficiary of recent funding trends has been 16–19 education (both in school sixth forms and in 16–19 further education). The four areas at the bottom of the figure address post-19 education, and show a smaller, but regular, increase in total nominal funding. A swap seems to be taking place, with increasing amounts of funding being channelled through the National Employer Training Programme, at the expense of 19+ FE, work-based learning and UfI funding for the delivery of learndirect

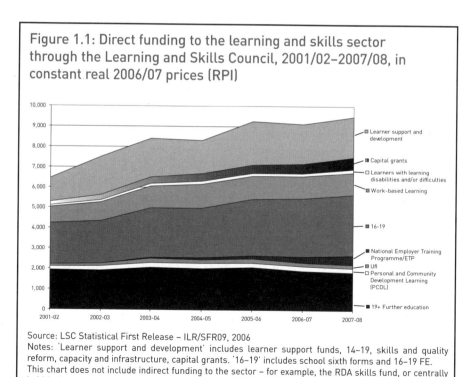

Figure 1.1: Direct funding to the learning and skills sector through the Learning and Skills Council, 2001/02–2007/08, in constant real 2006/07 prices (RPI)

Source: LSC Statistical First Release – ILR/SFR09, 2006
Notes: 'Learner support and development' includes learner support funds, 14–19, skills and quality reform, capacity and infrastructure, capital grants. '16–19' includes school sixth forms and 16–19 FE. This chart does not include indirect funding to the sector – for example, the RDA skills fund, or centrally held budgets, such as the QCA and SSDA. Figures for 2005/06, 2006/07 and 2007/08 reflect latest plans, and 2006/07 and 2007/08 include additional funding announced in the 2006 Budget. The LSC became responsible for sixth form funding in 2002/03 and for the whole Education Maintenance Allowance budget in 2005/06. 'UfI' (the organisation behind learndirect) covers UfI participation funding and, from 2004/05, UfI administration. The UfI figure for 2001/02 is an estimate only.

courses. The relatively small budget for personal and community develop-ment learning initiated an early downward move from 2004/05. It has now been frozen, in nominal terms, indicating a real terms decrease. The same trend applies to funds going to Ufi Ltd.

At the same time, it is important to keep in mind that only a small pro-portion of adult learning takes place within the public sector. There is a large commercial private sector operating in areas where employers and individuals invest their own resources, as well as formal and informal on-the-job training. Total employer training expenditure in 2005 was estimated at £33.3 billion a year in 2004/05 (LSC 2006a). This figure may be exag-gerated, as most of it comprises the wage costs of employees who are being trained, but nevertheless a total of around £2.4 billion was still spent on fees to external providers of off-the-job training.

In comparison, the LSC spends a maximum of £5 billion on post-19 education (including learner support and capital investment). Publicly sub-sidised adult learning forms only one part of what is taking place, and this has implications for the overall system.

Adult learning in England

Compared to other countries, England has a relatively high take-up of adult learning. However, those who are disadvantaged tend to participate less, thus reinforcing social and economic inequalities.

Participation in adult learning

Figure 1.2 shows the percentage of 25- to 64-year-olds in the labour force who participated in continuing education within a 12-month period in 2003, in 13 OECD countries. The UK ranked fifth, with 38 per cent participation – behind the Scandinavian countries and Switzerland. Although US figures for this measure are not available, the United States usually tends to rank above the UK on related measures such as participation rate for non-formal job-related continuing education and training (OECD 2005c, Chart C6.2b).

Indicators that separate out participation in formal and non-formal edu-cation provide broadly similar rankings (OECD 2005a, Chart C6.1). The same is true when looking at student enrolment in public and private insti-tutions, which suggests that participation in learning among the overall pop-ulation approximately reflects that of employees (OECD 2005a, Table C1.2).

However, the UK fares less well when it comes to time spent in training. In 2002, the UK ranked only ninth on hours of training and eighth on train-ing expenditure per employee across the 15 European Union countries, behind France and the Nordic countries (Leitch 2005). It should be noted that international comparisons of participation in learning tell us nothing about the quality or level of training, nor of the incidence of statutory

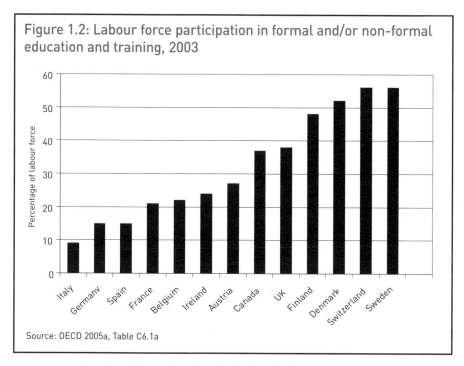

Figure 1.2: Labour force participation in formal and/or non-formal education and training, 2003

Percentage of labour force

Categories (left to right): Italy, Germany, Spain, France, Belgium, Ireland, Austria, Canada, UK, Finland, Denmark, Switzerland, Sweden

Source: OECD 2005a, Table C6.1a

courses, such as health and safety in England, for example.

Participation rates in England are likely to match these UK-wide trends. They are broadly equivalent in the other nations of the UK, although participation in Scotland has fallen in the past few years, with 36 per cent participation, compared to 43 per cent in England and 41 per cent in Wales, according to the Adult Participation in Learning Surveys carried out by the National Institute for Adult and Continuing Education (NIACE) (Aldridge and Tuckett 2006a)[1]. In England, participation in learning has remained broadly constant over the past decade, with around 40 per cent of adults having participated in some learning activity during the three years prior to the surveys (ibid). However, the very wide definition of learning used in the survey may not allow us to pick up on all the trends.

Indeed, there have been significant changes in participation in public provision, and these reflect directly the changes in funding mentioned previously. Figure 1.3 shows the number of learners of different ages who were enrolled on LSC-funded FE provision. A demographic surge in the 16 to 19 population has led to a significant increase of 16- to 19-year-old learners. In contrast, the number of 19- to 59-year-old learners in FE, which had

---

1. The OECD, NIACE and the Local Area Labour Force Survey (LLFS) all produce different surveys, with slightly different questions. Participation rates vary depending on a more or less comprehensive definition of learning (the main categories of formal, non-formal and informal being themselves subject to interpretation).

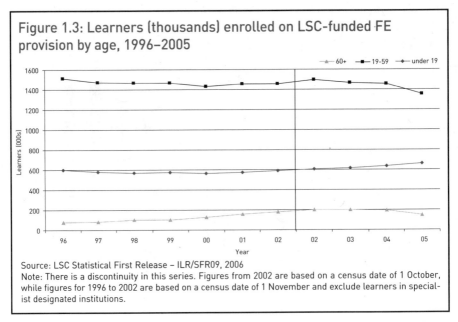

Figure 1.3: Learners (thousands) enrolled on LSC-funded FE provision by age, 1996–2005

Source: LSC Statistical First Release – ILR/SFR09, 2006

Note: There is a discontinuity in this series. Figures from 2002 are based on a census date of 1 October, while figures for 1996 to 2002 are based on a census date of 1 November and exclude learners in specialist designated institutions.

peaked in 2002, decreased by 9.7 per cent between 2002 and 2005. The number of people aged over 60 fell by 27.2 per cent between 2003 and 2005.

The same trends are likely to explain the increase by 9.7 per cent between 2002 and 2005 in full-time full-year participation (most likely to take place among those aged under 19), and the substantial 13 per cent decrease of part-time participation (most favoured by those over 25).

Improving participation of 16- to 19-year-olds is an important objective, and it is right for the Government to consider it as one of its priorities. However, because 16–19 provision is funded out of the same budget as other adult learning provision, it appears too often that this is at the expense of adult learners. Looking forward, it is important to remember that in an ageing population, people are expected to work and retire later and so will need to continue training well beyond their initial education.

Unequal access to adult learning

While participation in England is relatively high, and has been stable over the past decade, closer examination shows that overall figures are strongly biased towards those from more advantaged backgrounds. The most disadvantaged – in terms of initial education, employment and income – are least likely to be involved in adult learning. The NIACE survey shows that in 2006, 58 per cent of those in socio-economic classes A and B had recently participated in learning, against 27 per cent of those in classes D and E (Aldridge and Tuckett 2006a).

Participation in later learning is strongly correlated with two factors: the

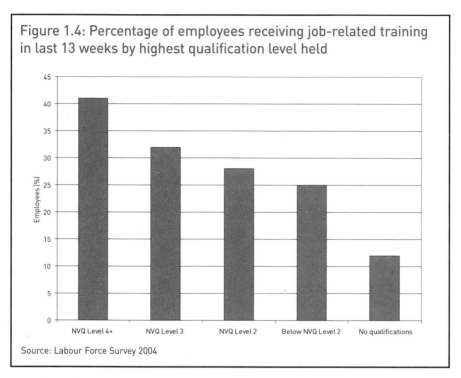

Figure 1.4: Percentage of employees receiving job-related training in last 13 weeks by highest qualification level held

Source: Labour Force Survey 2004

number of years spent in initial education, and the level of highest qualification achieved. Both factors indicate that the people who are most likely to leave education soon after the end of compulsory school with low or no qualifications are significantly less keen to sign up to learning. They are also less likely to receive training from employers. As Figure 1.4 shows, according to the Labour Force Survey, 42 per cent of those qualified to degree level or equivalent had received training in the previous 13 weeks, compared to just 12 per cent of those without qualifications in 2004.

Participation in later learning is also strongly linked to activity status. In 2006, around half of part-time workers (55 per cent), full-time workers (51 per cent) and registered unemployed adults (47 per cent) were current or recent learners, compared with 30 per cent of those who were not working (inactive) and 16 per cent of retired adults (Aldridge and Tuckett 2006a).

Women are more likely to take up learning in their own time and participate significantly more than men in public-sector provision (comprising 61 per cent of the total number of public-sector learners in 2005 according to LSC data). Surveys integrating private and public forms of learning tend to show a slightly more balanced picture. One 2006 survey found 44 per cent of women participating compared with 41 per cent of men (Aldridge and Tuckett 2006a). Although women are catching up with men, they have been traditionally less likely to receive training from their employers.

The same survey found that other groups were particularly under-represented in adult learning, including those with work-limiting disabilities, people on benefits, members of some minority ethnic groups (particularly British people of Asian origin) and those aged over 50.

Conclusions

The UK enjoys relatively high international standing in terms of adult learning, but the figures are misleading. Inequalities in access suggest that in the UK, those who are most disadvantaged benefit least from learning in later life.

The same trends are at work in other countries – for example, in Sweden, too, early school leavers are significantly less likely to access further education and training than their graduate counterparts. However, adult learning needs to be examined in the wider societal and labour market context. In England, adult learning follows on from relatively low levels of participation in 16–19 education and training. Inequalities also tend to be more pronounced than in other comparable European countries – particularly those in Scandinavian.

This means that in the UK, initial socio-economic disadvantage has a major bearing on educational achievement. In turn, levels of education have a disproportionate impact on labour market outcomes, such as wages and the chances of being in employment (Esping-Andersen 2005).

Although changes to the education and training system are unlikely to resolve these contradictions by themselves, they have a role to play. Adult learning, often dubbed 'second chance education' can also help those who missed out the first time round, but it is not clear that the Government's current policy for adult learning is the best way of addressing these needs.

2. The objectives of adult learning

There is some consensus about the main objectives for adult learning. The Independent Committee of Enquiry on adult learning (NIACE 2005) identified the following three:

- Access to employability
- Workforce development
- Creating and sustaining cultural value.

These objectives broadly echo the rationales set out by the Government in its latest Skills White Paper (DfES/DTI/HMT/DWP 2005: 5):

> 'Skills are central to achieving our national goals of prosperity and fairness. They are an essential contributor to a successful, wealth creating economy. They help businesses become more productive and profitable. They help individuals achieve their ambitions for themselves, their families and their communities.'

What is much more controversial is the relative importance given to these objectives, and the question of how they should influence the provision of adult learning. The Government frequently refers to social justice and the benefits for individuals, but its overriding concern now is on how skills can contribute to economic growth. This explains the shift in resources away from adult and community learning on to vocational provision – and is used to justify the growing tendency to direct resources towards training defined by employers.

The benefits of learning to the economy and to individuals are clearly linked: well-rounded people with a range of skills and an appetite to learn can reduce the costs of social exclusion, improve employment rates and help businesses. This, in turn, may contribute to economic prosperity. However, it does not follow that education driven directly by macro-economic objectives has the best chances of promoting the welfare both of the individual and of the nation. For someone with low-level skills, adult learning may offer low direct economic returns but important personal and social ones. For someone with high-level skills, the benefits may be reversed.

This means that a better balance needs to be achieved between the different objectives. An adult learning policy may need to start with the learner, rather than the economy, in order to be successful.

Macro-economic and fiscal objectives

One of the Government's main concerns in relation to skills policy is that the relatively high proportion of the UK workforce with low skills hampers the country's productivity. Businesses cannot find people with the skills that would help them improve their productive process and escape the 'low skills equilibrium' in which they are trapped. Improving the nation's supply of skills is expected to lead to better business practices and to economic growth. However, it is not clear that businesses' poor productivity is exclusively linked to a lack of available skills, nor that improving the stock of skills would automatically lead to better productivity.

The UK's low skills and occupational profile

The Government's concern with the impact of low skills on productivity is largely based on international comparisons that show that the UK, although well endowed with people with higher-level qualifications, has significantly fewer at intermediate level, and more with low or no qualifications, than other countries. However, international comparisons of skill levels need to be treated with caution. They are based on different qualification systems, which means that they often do not compare like with like (Keep 2006).

Using qualifications as a proxy for skills is also problematic, as many people have skills that are not accredited by qualifications (Macleod 2005), or have skills and qualifications that are not used in their current jobs – for example, graduates in jobs for which they are over-qualified. Even if qualifications are not used in the job itself, simply having them may help an individual to get a better job, because employers see that the candidate has a particular set of skills (a theory known as 'signalling' or 'screening'). Thus, some qualifications, particularly academic ones, may help in candidate selection, but without necessarily improving the UK's productivity.

When looking at the kinds of jobs that are available in the UK, rather than at the skills and qualifications of the workforce, it appears that the levels required in the labour market have remained remarkably constant over the past 20 years.

Table 2.1 shows that there has been a steady increase in the share of employment in the 'higher' managerial, professional and technical occupations, a greater proportion of which tend to demand qualifications at level 4 (degree equivalent) and above. At the other end of the spectrum, there has been a smaller decline of the overall share of 'lower' occupations. But the sharp decline in manual jobs has been partly offset by rising employment in the personal services and sales occupations (particularly retailing and care). It is the share of 'intermediate' occupations, with qualifications typically at levels 2 or 3, that has shown the fastest decline (Robinson 2001).

Research into the skills that are used effectively at work confirms that the

Table 2.1: Changes in the occupational structure of employment, 1984–2020					
	% of total employment				
	1984	1994	2004	2020 (estimate)	Average gross hourly earnings (2003) UK av. = 100
1. Managers and senior officials	12	14	15	17	160
2. Professional	8	10	12	14	149
3. Associate professional and technical	10	12	14	15	114
'Higher occupations'	30	36	41	46	
4. Admin/clerical/secretarial	5	15	13	11	75
5. Skilled trades	16	14	11	10	81
'Intermediate occupations'	31	29	24	21	
6. Personal services	4	6	8	9	60
7. Sales/customer services	6	7	8	9	62
8. Plant and machine operatives	12	10	8	7	69
9. Elementary occupations	16	14	11	8	60
'Lower occupations'	38	37	35	33	

Source: Leitch 2005, Table 3.1, with additional data from ippr

UK has more jobs requiring low qualifications than people to fill them. Whereas in 2001 there were only 2.9 million economically active people aged between 20 and 60 who possessed no qualifications, there remained 6.5 million jobs for which no qualification was required to obtain them (Felstead *et al* 2002). In contrast, there are more people with intermediate qualifications than jobs that require them. At higher levels, there is a better match between qualifications and jobs, with supply roughly equalling demand.

This picture is confirmed by the National Employers Skills Survey 2005 (LSC 2006a). It shows that in 2005 only a small minority of employers (7 per cent) had been affected by hard-to-fill vacancies since 2001, and only half of them attributed their recruitment problems to difficulties in finding suitably skilled candidates. The survey also shows that in the same year only 6 per cent of the total workforce were described as not being fully proficient (reflecting 'skills gaps').

Evidence of the 'excess supply of skills' and of the low incidence of skills shortages contradicts the more familiar claims that the needs of the economy are not being met. This may be due to factors other than the mere supply of skills. In terms of volume, lower-level occupations, such as personal services, sales and customer services, appear to pose the greatest recruitment challenges (LSC 2006a).

In many cases, this is likely to be caused more by job characteristics than by a lack of sufficiently qualified people in the workforce. Poor pay and conditions, such as shift work, is likely to deter the more suitable potential candidates from applying. This suggests that skills policy itself may not be able to do much to address the 'skills' problems reported by employers.

Basic skills

A possible explanation for the paradox of an excess supply of skills is that, despite having qualifications, the workforce might not have the appropriate skills required by the economy. The Confederation of British Industry (CBI) regularly complains that school leavers, and even graduates, lack basic skills in numeracy and literacy and are unable to work in teams or communicate appropriately with customers (CBI 2006).

There is certainly a problem with basic skills in the UK. People who are unable to read, write or add up properly face serious barriers in gaining employment and dealing with many aspects of their personal lives.

However, the proportion of people who are seriously affected by this problem may have been exaggerated. The Department for Education and Skills (DfES) Skills for Life Survey estimated that in 2002/03 no fewer than 26 million people, or 74 per cent of the working-age population, had levels of literacy and numeracy below those expected of school leavers (level 2 – equivalent to five GCSEs at grades A* to C). However, this figure is pulled up by the high number of people with low numeracy levels. When looking solely at literacy, the proportion is less, at 55 per cent of the working-age population (DfES 2003).

This implies that everyone without a grade A* to C GCSE in English and maths cannot read, write or add up properly, but this is clearly an overstatement, according to the former Director of the Basic Skills Agency, Alan Wells (Wells 2006). In fact, equating adult qualifications with key stages in schools is generally problematic because measures in school assess mastery of the curriculum, rather than skills. Measuring adult skills in terms of school key stages has led to an overestimation of the number of people without the skills necessary to function adequately in their jobs. It has also had practical repercussions. In one example, it resulted in resources for the Skills for Life programme, that were meant to address these basic skills problems not being directed towards those who needed them most (see Chapter 3).

In summary, skills play an important role in the economic output, but the relationship between the population's stock of skills, the way they are used by businesses, and economic productivity is more complex than usually implied. It also appears that adults and employers working at lower levels have few incentives to train. A better way of looking at this issue is to focus on the benefits that adult learning can bring to individuals.

Better labour market outcomes for individuals

There are clear benefits for individuals from gaining qualifications, both in terms of their wages and of their chances of getting jobs. These benefits vary widely depending on the type of qualifications and the individuals who take them.

Wage premiums for qualifications

Many educational qualifications attract significant and sizeable returns in the labour market. These benefits have remained relatively stable throughout the past decade, except for the disappearance of returns from very low-grade GCSEs (Sianesi 2003). However, Table 2.2 shows that there are considerable variations between different types of qualifications. The wage premium attached to having between one and four O levels or higher-grade GCSEs indicates that even a small number of GCSEs at grades A–C (which would be insufficient to reach level 2), offers a fairly good reward in the labour market.

This suggests that the Government's focus on level 2 may be too narrow. Additionally, the government policy to get more people on to level 2 qualifications has been strongly biased towards NVQs, as the requirement to

Table 2.2: Average wage premium (%) from obtaining qualifications		
Qualification	Men	Women
CSEs/lower GCSEs	ns	ns
1–4 O levels/higher GCSEs	14	11
5+ O levels/higher GCSEs	24	21
AS levels	ns	ns
1 A level	5	7
2+ A levels	15	14
First degree	24	25
Higher degree	13	15
Professional qualifications	36	40
Nursing	8	16
Teaching	7	26
Level 1 or 2 NVQ	ns	ns
Levels 3 to 5 NVQ	3	4
C&G Craft	7	ns
C&G Advanced	4	ns
ONC/ONC BTEC National	10	5
HND/HNC	13	9

Sources: Sianesi 2003 and Dearden *et al* 2004

Notes: ns = not statistically significant

The wage premiums are additive (so, for example, a man with 5+ O levels or higher GCSEs and 2+ A levels and a first degree will earn 63 per cent more than a man with no qualifications).

Controls are made for age, ethnicity, region, workplace size and public versus private sector.

register for a full level 2 tends to rule out an academic route. However, on average, NVQs offer no benefit to most recipients (Dearden *et al* 2004). Other vocational qualifications – BTECs in particular – do offer good wage premiums, though some (City and Guilds certificates) only for men. Separate research on basic skills shows that those taking literacy and numeracy courses do not appear to gain any extra leverage in the labour market (Machin *et al* 2001).

Low or negative premiums may be explained by the fact that these qualifications are taken mainly by people with characteristics that make them less attractive to employers in any case: low skill levels, poor employment history, or a disability (Dearden *et al* 2004). But looking at aggregates of wage premiums by skills levels may be unhelpful, as rewards differ widely between sectors and the types of individuals that take them.

Some sub-groups do earn significant positive returns from levels 1 and 2 NVQs – particularly low-ability individuals and those from poor family backgrounds (Dearden *et al* 2004). Additionally, a level 2 NVQ can provide a stepping stone to level 3, which does carry a wage premium, although relatively few people actually manage to make this progression.

Having a level 2 NVQ does also have a significant positive effect on the earnings of women in the health and social care sectors, where government regulations require training, which thus constitutes a form of licence to practise. Overall, men earn a negative premium from level 2 NVQs, with the exception of male plant and machine operatives (mostly in manufacturing). There are big negative premiums in the banking, insurance and finance sectors, both for men and women, and zero premiums in distribution, hotels and catering for men and women alike (Sianesi 2003). Again, this is largely due to the self-selection of those taking NVQs in these sectors.

Looking specifically at adult learning, there appears to be no clear additional gain in income from qualifications acquired as an adult at anything below degree level (Jenkins and Wolf 2005). However, gaining qualifications later in life may improve the incomes of low-attaining individuals compared to their peers who do not achieve such qualifications.

Improving employment

While several qualifications thus seem to offer relatively little in the way of wage premiums, levels of employment do indicate that there are benefits from acquiring skills and qualifications. Generally, those who hold any level 2 qualifications (including NVQs) are less at risk of being unemployed, and this is particularly true of the more vulnerable groups (Dearden *et al* 2004). This remains true for those who take their qualifications as adults (Jenkins and Wolf 2005).

Table 2.3 shows the employment probabilities of 23- to 25-year-olds in 2002, according to the qualifications that they had when they left school and those that they acquired later on (McIntosh 2004). It clearly indicates the employment benefits derived from acquiring later qualifications for those who left school without any qualification – both for men and for women. Every additional level of qualification brings in extra chances of being in employment (except for the small number of men who achieve above level 3 after they have left full-time education). This remains true even when using panel data to control for unobserved individual characteristics (which could make individuals who gain a qualification more likely to get a job irrespective of the qualification), and to ensure that the qualification is acquired before employment is attained.

The same trend is clear for those who left school with few or low GCSEs (level 1), with five GCSEs at grades A* to C (level 2) or with A levels (level 3). However, there are some unexplained disparities between the gains from each additional level of qualification. For men with an initial level 1, an additional qualification at level 2 brings substantial benefits over gaining just a level 1, but this is not replicated at other levels. For women, the picture is reversed: they are more likely to be in employment with each additional level of qualification, except at level 2. This may be partly due to

Table 2.3: Employment probabilities for 23- to 25-year-olds, by qualification combinations			
	Employment rate (%)		
	Men	Women	
No school qualifications			
+ none	68.2	30.6	
+ vocational level 1	75.3	58.3	
+ vocational level 2	88.7	70.3	
+ vocational level 3	94.3	77.4	
+ above level 3	77.9	93.5	
Lower or 1–4 higher GCSEs (level 1)			
+ none	80.8	56.4	
+ vocational level 1	80.6	66.3	
+ vocational level 2	91.4	66.0	
+ vocational level 3	88.9	86.8	
+ above level 3	82.2	91.1	
5+ higher GCSEs (level 2)			
+ none	88.3	76.8	
+ vocational level 1	92.9	73.6	
+ vocational level 2	93.5	81.2	
+ vocational level 3	92.4	86.8	
+ above level 3	90.5	92.1	
A levels (level 3)			
+ none	94.4	83.9	
+ vocational level 1	91.5	90.6	
+ vocational level 2	94.8	78.0	
+ vocational level 3	95.8	90.5	
+ above level 3	91.6	92.0	
Source: McIntosh 2004 using data from **Labour Force Survey 2002**			

differences in the sectors in which men and women work and seek qualifications – a link that needs to be further explored.

Acquiring skills and qualifications as an adult can thus bring clear benefits – particularly for disadvantaged groups – and these benefits are more substantial with regard to employment than wages. This may have implications for the Government's 'welfare to work' policies, which have concentrated on getting people back into jobs as soon as possible, rather than helping them improve their skills.

Better outcomes for individuals, the family and the community

Adult learning can result in outcomes for individuals that are wider than simply improving their position in the labour market or business performance, and social justice provides a strong rationale for making these opportunities available to adults who did not access them in their initial education. However, it also requires one to take a wider perspective on the learning and upskilling process that includes, but goes beyond, an exclusive focus on qualification attainment.

The wider benefits of learning

One would expect education to be linked to wider personal and social outcomes, such as better health, reduced crime and increased social cohesion. It is often noted that adult learning can help people cope with personal finance, fight social exclusion, gain confidence and improve their well-being. Nevertheless, hard evidence for such effects of adult learning can be difficult to come by. Much of the research on educational outcomes (other than those relating to the labour market) is of a qualitative nature.

Focusing on outcomes that are often difficult to quantify, this research often has to rely on qualitative surveys, interviews and case studies. As a result, it may be hard to establish that there is a causal effect, rather than a mere association, between learning and outcomes. Similarly, establishing value for money may be difficult, as personal and social benefits cannot always be costed.

However, research on the wider benefits of learning provides some robust evidence on a small and specific, but important, range of indicators. Generally, education has been recognised as having benefits on health, crime and social cohesion (Feinstein 2002a, 2002b, Preston and Feinstein 2004). Some of the outcomes that have been demonstrated specifically for adult learning are presented in Box 2.1.

Although the outcomes shown in Box 2.1 focus on specific indicators, they are sufficiently significant to show that adult learning brings benefits not only to individuals and their communities but also to the society at large, by helping to reduce costs – particularly those related to ill health.

Box 2.1: Wider outcomes associated with adult learning

- Allowing for background characteristics, 24 per cent of smokers who took no course quit by age 42. Taking one or two courses brings this percentage up to 27.3 per cent, which represents an increase in the chances of giving up by a factor of well over one-eighth (Feinstein 2002b).
- Almost half (45 per cent) of adults who took between three and 10 courses increased their level of exercise between 33 and 42, compared to just 38 per cent of adults with the same characteristics who did not take any course. This represents an increase in the chances of taking more exercise by a factor of almost one-fifth (ibid).
- Participation in leisure courses can significantly increase inter-racial tolerance (Preston and Feinstein 2004).
- 14 per cent of adults who took one or two leisure courses increased their memberships between the ages of 33 and 42, as compared to the predicted 9 per cent of adults with similar characteristics who took no course of any type (Feinstein 2002b).

The Government is engaged in several attitude-changing campaigns to encourage people to give up smoking, eat healthily, and exercise. Schemes have been launched to fight racism, encourage voluntary and community involvement, and raise environmental awareness.

Meanwhile, social policies try, for example, to strengthen patient voices in health, integrate offenders back into society, and help people negotiate housing or financial arrangements. The research on the wider benefits of learning shows that adult education should be considered an integral part of all these strategies.

The research also demonstrates that these wider benefits of learning are not linked exclusively to qualification attainment. Participating in a learning activity and engaging with other learners and, particularly, the teacher are all essential factors in bringing about the desired outcomes. Similarly, leisure and community courses may sometimes have as much of an impact on these outcomes as vocational training (Preston and Feinstein 2004).

More equal life chances

The number of years spent in education, and the level of attainment, are closely linked to social mobility. This is measured by labour market outcomes. As seen in relation to wage premiums, the evidence does not show that qualifications obtained as an adult under degree level have any impact on wages, and thus do not seem to lead to social mobility. This explains why government policy and resources concentrate on early years and tackling child poverty.

However, research shows that the efforts need to be sustained at later stages of people's lives in order to maintain the momentum of early years and school policies, if the benefits are not to be lost (Delorenzi *et al* 2005). This is particularly true when people enter, and try to progress in, the labour market – points at which socio-economic background seems to regain importance.

Social justice also pleads for a healthy provision of adult learning for those who have been disadvantaged as children and teenagers. In England, the variation between pupils' attainment at school is among the highest in Europe, with a very strong correlation between educational achievement and socio-economic background. In the last quarter of a century, inter-generational mobility has fallen in the UK, so that family background matters more today than it did in the past (Blanden *et al* 2005).

This means that there is a strong case for offering 'second-chance' education to those who missed out in the first place – often the very people who get fewer chances to train as adults. This means supporting adult learning that enhances the chances of being in employment and promotes the measurable and non-measurable wider benefits of learning. The rationales provided by social justice, and the wider benefits of learning, point to the needs for an adult learning system that targets support at the more disadvantaged in society, while offering a relatively wide choice of courses.

Is the current adult learning system fit for purpose?

Despite its rhetoric, the Government has increasingly narrowed down its adult learning policy to part of one objective – increasing overall economic productivity. This is in contrast with policies in Scotland and Wales, for example, which constantly emphasise dual goals: economic competitiveness and social justice (Byrne and Raffe 2005). Considering that adult learning is unlikely (in the absence of other major reforms in the labour market and economy) to lead to the expected massive rise in performance, this policy might be counter-productive. Increasingly designed to fulfil an exclusively economic objective, the system does not work efficiently, and some groups are losing out – including some of the most disadvantaged.

Meeting the objectives for adult learning
Much of the rationale and reform principles of the Skills Strategy were present under the successive Conservative governments and, in a slightly toned down version, in the first term of the Labour government. However, it has been no less difficult to show an independent effect of adult learning (and education generally) on productivity than it has on health and social cohesion (Tamkin *et al* 2004, Tamkin 2005).

Programmes designed with an exclusive economic focus in mind have tended to sideline the learner, or potential learner. Much effort is devoted to 'putting employers in the driving seat' – a move that the Leitch Review of Skills wants to push even further (Leitch 2006). But experience so far does not suggest that involving employers in programme and qualification design has improved the recognition and wage premiums attached to these qualifications.

What is more, this policy has often led to resources being redirected towards employers and employer bodies (for example, through Train to Gain or the Sector Skills for Business Network), which would be better used if targeted at individual learners. It is also worth remembering that many employers do not build training into their business planning. It seems risky to try to fund adult learning via such employers. Also, doing so does nothing to help individuals who are currently unemployed, in temporary jobs or experiencing a succession of short-lived jobs.

There is also an economic case underlying this redefinition of priorities. Reductions in benefit payments, healthcare costs and social injustice would be beneficial for society, and for the economy, as a whole. Although the final report of the Leitch Review gives equal weight to every level of skills, this conclusion chimes with its interim report, which showed that investing in basic literacy and numeracy skills produces the biggest benefit relative to cost, compared to intermediate and higher-level skills.

How the system operates

The adult learning system has experienced a number of radical shifts. Marketisation in the early 1990s was followed by the rhetoric of lifelong learning, increase in resources and central planning of Labour's first two terms in government. The Government has now moved back to budget restrictions that link public spending to the sector's capacity to provide skills for the economy, and a push towards introducing more market-like mechanisms, such as increasing competition between providers. Unsurprisingly, this has created significant instability in the sector.

Aside from the competitive agenda, government policy remains heavily geared towards identifying skill needs and planning for the system to deliver them, in collaboration with employers. However, as the interim report for the Leitch Review highlighted, it is very difficult to predict the rise of technologies such as IT, or the types of jobs that will be important in the future. National workforce planning has a poor record, and trying to ensure central provision of the skills that the Government or employer bodies believe to be necessary is doomed to failure (Leitch 2005). This suggests a need for a system that emphasises flexibility and user choice.

The two PSA targets for basic skills and level 2 have focused attention on numbers going through the system and qualification attainment. Both are clearly important. However, more attention needs to be devoted to the quality of education and training.

Targeting resources

Resources are limited but, given the recent increases and national budget requirements, it would be difficult to argue for significant additional spending in the short term. However, existing resources could be used more efficiently, and need to be focused on the people and organisations that need them most. Up to now, the system has tended to provide significant subsidy to relatively well-off learners, and a degree of redistribution needs to take place. At the same time, it is necessary to safeguard an appropriate structure offering provision to a wider group of fee-paying and partly subsidised learners.

Some groups of adults are currently losing out – in particular:

- Those on low incomes but with no need for basic skills or a full level 2 qualification
- The unemployed, who often get fewer chances to re-train than those in employment
- The economically inactive, including mothers who would like to return to work or need to break social isolation, and disadvantaged older learners.

The needs of these groups need to be better taken into account.

Conclusions

In summary, the following principles for reform and policy implications can be drawn from the analysis above:

A new rationale for adult learning

What is required is a clear rationale for adult learning that provides a better balance between the different sets of objectives, and that starts in the right · place: with the learner. This rationale needs to accompany technological and organisational change in the economy and society, so that employers and individuals can acquire new skills as and when they feel the need for them. It needs to help those who are unemployed or economically inactive to come back into employment and those with low attainment to improve their position in the labour market. It also needs to help those who are most disadvantaged to gain confidence, take up new opportunities, and integrate into their communities and wider society.

Public service provision and targeted support

Government subsidy for adult learning needs to ensure two things: first, that priority groups can easily access an appropriate range of learning options that are relevant both for employment and for social or personal improvement skills and, second, that everyone, including employers, has access to affordable, quality provision, for which they will have to share some or most of the cost.

This distinction is important because resources need to be redistributed towards those who are worst off, and who require additional fee subsidies and/or financial support. The same logic means that public resources need to be more fairly distributed across all areas of post-19 learning – particularly between higher and further education. At the same time, it is important that we do not move towards segregated systems where different providers cater for the needs of each group. This is why the Government needs to have an overview of the overall system.

A learner-led and learning-led system

Despite all the rhetoric about putting employers at the centre of the system, the main focus of learning remain the individuals who are expected to acquire new skills and knowledge as a result of the process. Learning requires their active involvement. If they have a say in the type of provision they engage in, they are more likely to choose courses that will benefit them, and should also get more out of their learning .

This suggests a different approach, focusing not so much on specific qualifications as on specific groups. Targeted groups should also have the right to choose what type of further education and training they wish to undertake, as in higher education, although some courses (such as in leisure or personal development) could receive a smaller subsidy.

The following chapters will now explore the policy implications of these broad principles in three areas:

- learning provision
- funding and financial support
- the institutional framework.

3. Adult learning, skills and qualifications

There is a broad consensus around the Government's desire to create a 'demand-led' system. However, when discussion begins about how this demand is to be defined, disagreements emerge. Does this 'demand' refer to the demand from individual adults, the demand from individual employers, or the aggregate demand expressed by labour market analysis and the Sector Skills Councils?

In recent years, labour market analysts and employers have increasingly been asked to define demand, through targets and programmes such as Train to Gain. But this may not match most people's understanding of a 'demand-led' system. Consequently, the Leitch Review of Skills has now recommended that individual employers and learners should be in the driving seat, and that by 2010 all public funding for adult vocational skills in England be routed through Train to Gain and Learner Accounts (Leitch 2006).

However, this approach tends to marginalise two crucial players: the learners themselves, who get little say within the Train to Gain programme, and the learning providers, who are best placed for interpreting demand in a given area.

The role of the Government is to encourage participation of disadvantaged groups and to make sure that a quality learning offer is reasonably accessible to all. The Government's main tools for shaping provision have been entitlements to free provision and targets, which force providers to focus on specific programmes. Both tools focus on qualifications.

Education policy in England is unusual in the central role that it allocates to formal and externally assessed qualifications. At all educational stages, tests and qualifications are used as a way of measuring students' understanding and skills, both to help them progress and, in some instances, for selection purposes. These assessments serve as major criteria in evaluating teacher, school and college performance, for accountability purposes. They determine the funding that learning providers receive and how they are allowed to use it. Through the national PSA targets, tests are also central in measuring the performance of the whole system.

Adult education policy is no exception, and it has become increasingly focused on two targets: strengthening the population's basic skills and increasing level 2 attainment. Both these targets require more people to fulfil the requirements of the relevant assessments and qualifications, in order to prove that they have reached the necessary level.

However, this focus on targets and qualifications raises a number of issues. Qualifications can be an important objective for individuals, and many will see benefits in acquiring them. However, in other cases – particularly at the lowest levels – qualification may discourage, rather than encourage, participation. It may also promote an instrumental view of teaching and learning – 'working to the test' – which runs counter to a real increase in skill levels. This highlights the need for careful analysis of the advantages and disadvantages of the system, and suggests that more flexibility might be necessary in the way qualifications are used. It is important to move away from limited accreditation of existing skills and to leave more space for the acquisition of new skills and for the learning process itself.

The impact of targets and entitlements

The two targets of strengthening basic skills and increasing level 2 attainment enjoy relatively wide support. They have helped focus attention on those with low educational attainment, who are mainly found in the most disadvantaged sections of the population. They also seem to respond to business complaints about the low levels of basic and general skills in the UK. However, they have led to increasingly narrow provision that may often fail to meet the requirments of those who need it most.

A number of programmes and initiatives have been launched in order to ensure that targets are met, as follows:

- Basic skills qualifications have been developed.
- Initiatives have been designed to improve the qualifications of teachers and lecturers.
- Entitlements to free tuition have been granted at the relevant levels.
- Some forms of financial support, such as the Adult Learning Grant, have been introduced, aimed at those studying towards these qualifications.
- Subsidies are now provided to employers that are prepared to help their staff train towards basic skills and level 2 qualifications, through Train to Gain.

Progress towards the two targets

The DfES claims to be on course to meet both targets (DfES 2006a). However, independent research shows that the level 2 target – to increase by 3.6 million the number of adults in the workforce qualified to at least level 2 by 2010 – will be difficult to achieve should existing trends continue (Macleod 2005). The interim target of 1 million more people with level 2 by 2006 was achieved, but the 2010 target requires a doubling of the former rate of attainment in order to be met.

The national rollout of Train to Gain could help move towards the target. However, the policies that were designed to help meet the target seem to have disproportionately helped those with the 'least distance to travel'. It appears that those in skilled occupations, and those holding some GCSEs but not enough for a level 2, are the most likely to progress towards achieving the target. These are often people who may have been working at a level equivalent to level 2, irrespective of their qualifications. Acquiring a qualification may be beneficial to some of them, despite the low wage premiums linked to such qualifications (as seen in Chapter 2), but these policies are unlikely to help those who need help most.

The basic skills target poses similar problems. It aims to improve the basic skill levels of 2.25 million adults between 2001 and 2010, with a milestone of 1.5 million by 2007. Programmes that were designed to meet the target may have often left those with the deepest skill deficiencies (who also tend to have the least inclination to participate) by the wayside.

Evaluations of the Skills for Life programme show that those most likely to take literacy and numeracy courses in colleges between 2002 and 2004 were 16- to 18-year-olds in full-time education (Meadows and Metcalf 2005, House of Commons Committee of Public Accounts 2006). It also appears that those with low qualifications are more likely to participate than those with no qualifications at all. Again, although these learners clearly need to improve their basic skills, resources have clearly been drawn towards those who are easiest to reach. More needs to be done to encourage participation among certain groups (Metcalf and Meadows 2004), including:

- those without qualifications
- those with particularly low competence in literacy and numeracy
- those with long-term disabilities or illnesses
- those with children.

The Leitch Review of Skills recommended that the Government be even more ambitious in its objectives and increase the number of adults with qualifications at each level: to up to 95 per cent for basic skills, 90 per cent for level 2, and 40 per cent for a level 4 qualification (Leitch 2006). Although the aspiration towards improving the skills of the whole population is legitimate, this seems to replicate some of the problems of the target number-based approach and to ignore the importance of quality of learning.

Without significantly more funding, PSA targets and entitlements to free tuition, it is also unlikely that the ambition to raise attainment at levels 3 and 4 will be met.

Entitlement to free tuition

Entitlement to free tuition at the relevant levels is a particularly significant policy tool to help towards the target. Accredited basic skills tuition has been free since 2001, and an entitlement to a first full level 2 qualification has been available across England since 2006. Additionally, this is being extended to an entitlement to a first full level 3 qualification up to the age of 25.

The level 2 entitlement offers free tuition to anyone who has not achieved five A* to C GCSEs or another level 2 qualification. The entitlement was introduced to help this target be reached, and is limited to provision leading to a first full qualification, at level 2 (or 3).

This is hard to reconcile with adults' patterns of learning: adults mainly learn part time, alongside their jobs, often in short spells. It is difficult for them to embark on a whole qualification, unless it is an NVQ assessed at work. Many adults already have a few GCSEs, and it would be worthwhile to allow them to pass a few more, rather than having to start a whole new vocational qualification. Meanwhile, others who already have a level 2 qualification might benefit from the opportunity to re-train in another sector.

Another significant constraint is that the entitlement does not apply to those who need to work towards a level 2 by starting at a lower level, whether at entry level or level 1. These are the learners with the greatest needs. Progressing and achieving a level 2 qualification may take them significantly more time than those who are closer to the target, but they stand to benefit most and should be able to access appropriate free provision in order to get there.

The Foundation Learning Tier, which will be introduced in 2007, is an attempt to bridge this gap. It will provide pathways based around personal and social development, key and basic skills, and vocational or subject-based learning at entry level or level 1 (Gamble 2006, QCA 2006a). If appropriately funded, the Foundation Learning Tier has the potential to introduce more flexibility and thus open up opportunities for those at lower levels.

Flexibility has also been introduced on the other side of the entitlement: if they are ready to work at that level, learners without a level 2 qualification are allowed to jump directly to a level 3 qualification. In addition, in 2006 a new entitlement to free tuition towards a first full level 3 qualification for those up to 25 years old was announced. These are important measures in freeing up the system, although they replicate some of the shortcomings of the level 2 entitlements, such as not recognising the benefits of completing a qualification that is already partially achieved.

Generally, defining the entitlement by level of study is problematic. As seen in Section 2, qualifications at level 2 can carry a wide range of premiums, depending on whether they are academic or vocational (level 1 GCSEs lead to higher wage premiums than most level 2 NVQs) and the sector in which they are taken. For example, the platform for employability might be level 2 in social care, but level 3 in electrical engineering.

It would be very difficult, and unproductive, to further refine the entitlement in order to reflect these differences. So, the best way to deal with the untidy nature of the labour market, and of adult learning, would be to introduce more flexibility within the system. People with low previous attainment should be allowed to study at the level, and in the pattern, that suits them most – and to study towards a qualification or not, as they wish.

Qualifications versus learning and skills

The importance of formal and externally assessed qualifications in English education policy means that significant resources are spent on certifying skills, rather than on the teaching and learning process. The benefits of this system are assumed to be the national validity granted to qualifications and the motivation that this gives to those who take them.

However, many organisations do not use qualification as a formal selection criterion (Jenkins and Wolf 2005), and the claim to national validity is undermined by the fact that employers know little about most vocational qualifications. The evidence also shows that many adults who would be willing to enrol on courses are deterred by, or do not seek, qualifications – and this is often true of their employers as well (Torrance and Coultas 2004, West 2004). In some cases, tests can precipitate dropout and deter progression – particularly for end-of-course summative tests.

The question of what is assessed, and how it is assessed, is very influential in determining what is taught and how it is taught, and it appears that all too often in outcomes-based programmes testing is allowed to take precedence over learning, in exactly the same way that 'teaching to the test' has become a problem in schools. This is particularly true of the two types of qualifications that are attached to the targets: basic skills and NVQs. As a result, testing may end up having a negative effect on the very outcome it is intended to promote – progression in learning and achievement (Torrance *et al* 2005).

Basic skills teaching and testing

Inspection of the Skills for Life programme suggests that, although it has been highly successful in increasing the number of learners of literacy, numeracy and English as a second language (ESOL), the quality of provision is much lower than in any other area of learning (Ofsted/ALI 2003). There are serious shortages of qualified and experienced teachers. Many of the learners with the greatest need – those in Jobcentre Plus provision, work-based learning and prison education – are with the providers that have the least qualified staff and the fewest resources (National Audit Office 2004). Not all providers have sufficient incentives to respond to the call from the DfES to improve the qualifications teachers of basic skills – particularly for those on temporary or part-time contracts.

A focus on clearly measurable outcomes may have acted as a distraction from the primary objective: to ensure a high-quality, motivating teaching and learning process. This may partly explain the low premiums attached to literacy and numeracy qualifications, as seen in Chapter 2. The labour market is unlikely to reward these courses if they grant only limited new skills.

Finally, research shows that basic skills are best learnt when they are linked to personal and practical requirements and embedded in other courses (NRDC 2005). However, a narrow focus on qualification attainment may work against this type of provision. Again, this suggests that more flexibility is required, and that there should be more incentives towards quality of provision. The new functional skills qualifications that are currently being developed are not meant to address these issues.

Assessing competence: the National Vocational Qualifications (NVQs)

The level 2 target and entitlement have NVQs at their core, and most of the programmes that are designed to achieve the target lead to NVQs. For example, the vast majority of those in the Employer Training Pilots (now called Train to Gain) were working towards an NVQ at level 2 (Hillage *et al* 2006).

However, a wide body of research has shown that NVQs have significant shortcomings (West 2004). NVQs were designed to assess competence in the workplace, and aim to accredit skills that are being acquired at work. As a result, the educational component is relatively marginal, and skills may be certified without any new learning actually taking place. In practice, the learning process has often been replaced by excessive and instrumental evidence gathering.

NVQs were designed to maximise choice and flexibility for learners, but this objective may be hampered by practical constraints. For example, people who do not have the chance to work in a particular area within their job will not be able to acquire the associated skills (Tennant *et al* 2005). Some NVQs are badly designed, and there is repetition across course units. What is more, NVQs are not designed to facilitate progression to higher levels, despite their unit-based structure. As a result, NVQs bring relatively few new skills – a fact that partly explains the low or non-existent wage premiums attached to them.

The premiums for NVQs in health and social care are the exception – precisely because they involve skill and knowledge acquisition, in order to meet the statutory requirements within this sector.

NVQs were mainly designed as a way of certifying people's skills. Signalling a person's competence was expected to improve their chances of finding a job, or of getting a better one. Instead it appears that, if anything, NVQs below level 3 only signal poor skills to employers. This calls into question the 'competence-based' approach to assessment within NVQs, and suggests that trying to trade off the more demanding teaching of new skills against merely certifying existing skills does not pay off.

Accrediting skills at work: the Employer Training Programme

The Leitch Review of Skills has recommended that most of the public funding for adult vocational skills is routed through Train to Gain (Leitch 2006). However, evaluations of the Employer Training Pilots (ETPs) have shown several of the problems that were associated both with outcome-related targets and with programmes that were focused almost exclusively on qualifications. The Leitch Review does not suggest any way of remedying these problems. Box 3.1 describes the main features of the programme.

Box 3.1: From the Employer Training Pilots to Train to Gain

A series of Employer Training Pilots was established in 2002, before the Train to Gain programme was rolled out nationally in 2006. Train to Gain aims to address UK employers' low involvement in training. As a core, it offers employers (LSC 2006b):

- a free skills brokerage service, to help identify employers' skills needs and put them in touch with appropriate training providers
- fully subsidised training, delivered at a time and place to suit the employer, for low skilled employees up to a first full level 2 qualification, and with support for progression to level 3
- free information, advice and guidance for employees
- for employers with less than 50 employees, wage compensation for the time that employees spend in training.

The following additional elements may be offered at regional or local level:

- grants for leadership and management training for small and medium enterprises
- support for Foundation Degrees, union learning representatives, 'skills coaches' and 'skills passports'.

The core offer broadly replicates the main features of the pilots, which also tested some variants. However, the skills brokerage offered as part of Train to Gain is now more explicitly targeted at 'harder to reach' employers, with a minimum of 51 per cent of targeted employers now in this category. This is following evaluations that showed significant deadweight: about 85 to 90 per cent of the training would have been provided by employers in any case (Abramovsky *et al* 2005).

The programme will receive £473 million in 2001–08, including £30 million for wage compensation and £36 for brokerage. It is expected to involve 52,000 employers and 235,000 employees per year.

The Employer Training Pilots were based on an 'assess-train-assess' model, designed to assess an individual's competence, train the person to meet their identified skill gaps, and then conduct a final assessment. In practice, however, only around half of learners had an initial training needs assessment, and a much lower proportion followed the full model (Hillage et al 2006).

An evaluation by the Adult Learning Inspectorate (ALI) confirmed that although this 'assess-train-assess' model is working well in most cases where it is used, it is most often replaced by an 'assess-assess-assess' approach, where learners' existing skills are simply accredited as a means of gaining an NVQ. The learners are not sufficiently challenged and do not get the opportunity to build on their existing skills and gain new ones (Ashton et al 2005). There is little – sometimes no – formal training involved. Assessors too often take it on themselves to build portfolios rather than giving the task to the learner, thus denying the individual the benefits that could at least be gained from reflecting on their own skills and working practices.

Again, efficiency and success in getting numbers through the assessment hoops seem to work to the detriment of real learning and skills acquisition.

Surveys of employers have shown high levels of satisfaction with the scheme (Hillage et al 2006). However, this is not surprising in a scheme offering free provision – especially when it replaces training that employers would normally have paid for. Employees also indicated high levels of initial satisfaction, although they tended to see fewer benefits as their involvement progressed. Few had much choice about what course they did, with around half saying that they had no choice at all. So the benefits were narrowly focused on people's current jobs, rather than giving them skills to do a different job, or to get a promotion or better pay.

The key question for Train to Gain is whether the benefits justify its high cost. In the absence of hard evidence showing improved wages and employability, the national rollout of such an expensive programme seems to have been premature.

Impact on other forms of provision

The focus imposed by targets on specific levels and qualifications means that other forms of provision have received a decreasing share of attention and resources. However, the fates of personal and community development learning, of level 3 and of HE provision in colleges differ from one another significantly.

Personal and community development learning
The main casualty of the Government's move away from lifelong learning has been personal and community development learning (PCDL), which

encompasses both what is often described as 'leisure learning' and 'first steps' provision. The latter is designed to encourage people to return to learning, usually with short, part-time courses in a wide and eclectic range of subjects, ranging from sport and recreation to IT and non-accredited courses in literacy, numeracy and English for speakers of other languages (LSC 2004).

Part of PCDL has been 'protected', with the Government committing to keep LSC spending within recent limits for the time being (DfES *et al* 2005). Local authorities are expected to take over this type of provision, for which they were already responsible until it was handed over to the LSC in 2001. Many providers have responded by changing their courses so that they lead to accredited and externally assessed qualifications – although this raises the questions about costs and the effects of testing mentioned earlier. Fees are also going up – particularly for leisure and personal development courses.

The main reason why this form of provision has been exposed to budget reductions is that it is difficult to prove any direct benefits, in terms of wages and employment, for those who enrol on the courses. Qualitative evaluations show high levels of learner satisfaction and social and personal benefits – particularly for older learners, returning mothers, disadvantaged communities and people who need to break from stress or loneliness (Morrell *et al* 2004). This form of provision has also been shown to attract people back into certificated and more formal learning (Denholm and Macleod 2003). Part of this form of provision can be considered 'leisure learning', although it is not always easy to draw a clear distinction between the two. So, for most of the population, learning that is most akin to leisure should be paid for by individuals, but it should be subsidised for disadvantaged groups. Access to this sort of provision should be protected for those priority groups that face multiple barriers to learning and have the greatest distance to travel towards engagement with learning, including those who do not have a level 2 qualification and are on low incomes. Although they should still be expected to progress to courses that may have a more direct labour market relevance, PCDL needs to be preserved as a point of entry.

From level 3 to higher education

Level 3 provision remains one of the Government's educational priorities, and significant steps are being taken to improve provision for young people. Post 19, level 3 provision is targeted mainly at younger adults, and is only free of charge up to the age of 25 with the new level 3 entitlement. There is some flexibility for those without a level 2 to benefit from the entitlement or Train to Gain directly at level 3. Beyond this, however, those without a level 3 qualification are largely expected to pay an increasing part of the cost for this provision.

Ultimately, an entitlement to free provision should be introduced for all those without a level 3. Those who have not benefited from free provision up to the age of 19 (or, now, 25) should still be able to get level 3 provision at the age of 26 or later. It makes sense to introduce the entitlement progressively, given current resource constraints. However, better financial arrangements need to be made now, in order to support those willing to study towards a level 3 qualification, whether full time or part time, including grants for the most disadvantaged – an issue that will be explored in the next section.

Financial arrangements are also crucial for those studying towards higher education (HE) qualifications (level 4) in further education institutions. This area has been protected because of the PSA target to get 50 per cent of 18- to 30-year-olds in HE by 2010. However, the growth in the mature student market for HE has slowed down, and is possibly saturated, because virtually all A level students now go into HE (Denholm and Macleod 2003). Flexible and part-time delivery, as well as provision closer to home, is crucial to widen participation and attract more disadvantaged students.

A learning-led system

The basic skills and level 2 targets and entitlements have been largely welcome as a way of focusing attention on disadvantaged groups that previously received little attention. However, they have been interpreted too narrowly, and have often failed to reach the most disadvantaged and to bring real gains to those whose newly acquired qualifications simply certified skills that they already had.

The focus should be not just on obtaining qualifications, but also on actually learning and acquiring new skills. There are many benefits to be drawn from engaging in the learning process itself – not least in developing social and personal skills. The most disadvantaged people need to have easy access to a choice of provision.

More choice for learners

The entitlements should be applied in a more flexible way, so that those who are entitled to free tuition can choose the forms of provision that suit them most. Some flexibility has already been introduced by allowing those without a level 2 qualification to jump directly to a full level 3, while the Foundation Learning Tier has the potential to open up options at lower levels. However, this will only be the case if the scheme is appropriately funded. In particular, it must be recognised that such courses often use additional support in the form of a teaching assistant. It will also have to be sufficiently adaptable for learners below level 2 to receive the personalised provision that they need. The degree of prescription for the combination of units should remain minimal.

The level 2 entitlement should also be made more flexible by allowing adults to take only partial qualifications when this enables them to complete an existing qualification – for example, by getting one or two additional GCSEs – and funding and financial arrangements need to make it easier for adults to take up part-time learning.

More flexibility should also be applied to the choice of qualifications and awards. Despite the shortcomings of NVQs, it would appear risky and costly to engage in another centralised attempt to design new qualifications to replace them.

The Leitch Review suggests giving Sector Skills Councils (SSCs) the responsibility to develop and approve vocational qualifications. The argument is that employers' current disinclination to train is due to their lack of trust in the qualification system (Leitch 2006). However, it is important to remember that employers (or rather employer bodies) have been heavily involved in developing qualifications – particularly the problematic NVQs, and it is not clear why an approach that starts with sector bodies defining National Occupational Standards should be more successful next time round. The fact that SSCs have not yet proved themselves would only make the process even more problematic (see Chapter 5).

An alternative is to give more space to awards that are not externally assessed. A body of qualifications that are rigorously specified, quality assured and nationally validated is important. But when the stakes are lower – for example, providing credit for learning rather than a passport to university – the qualifications could be more flexible and locally devised.

There is a wide range of options, on a continuum ranging from purely internal and college awards, through Open College Network (OCN)-accredited qualifications, to qualifications built around units in the Qualifications and Credit Framework. In many countries it is institutions, rather than awarding bodies, that award qualifications. The Further Education Bill will give colleges the power to award their own Foundation Degrees. This will be an important test of how this system can work at lower levels.

As one example, the OCN offers a mechanism that allows awards devised in colleges to be more widely recognised, through a peer review process. Assessment is carried out in-house but is moderated by the OCN, which ensures that standards are established and maintained.

College awards and OCN-accredited provision alike would both have major benefits, in that they would reduce the costs of accreditation, which should be redirected towards better quality provision. Provision that is not accredited by the Qualifications and Curriculum Authority (QCA) would not be synonymous with a lack of accountability. It would still have to be properly inspected in order to check its quality – as is the case with accredited provision, which is not always a guarantee of quality teaching. The OCN would also allow lecturers and learning providers to design their own programmes and tests, rather than merely asking them to train students towards given qualifications.

Such an approach would prove motivational both for learners and their tutors. It would allow teaching to be adapted more closely to the needs of particular students, would empower the profession, and might help solve some of the image and recruitment difficulties currently encountered. There are excellent examples of such qualifications already existing in colleges (for example, see Newham College's NewCad, described in Delorenzi and Robinson 2005).

The Qualifications and Credit Framework (QCF), which is currently being developed, offers the perspective of going one step further than OCN-accredited provision, by allowing learners to combine externally accredited units. This framework aims to bring together units from all qualifications, at all levels. Learning providers would be able to build up externally assessed qualifications, giving credits to learners as they accumulate units towards a full qualification. This has the potential to create the flexibility required for adult learners, enabling them to build qualifications progressively and to move between different pathways, by being able to carry units with them (QCA 2006b).

However, as with the Foundation Learning Tier, this framework will only lead to genuine improvement if it remains very flexible at the point of use, allowing real personalisation of learning. This means that the 'rules of combination' defined by the QCA would have to be kept to a minimum.

Strict definitions of entitlements and funding limited to externally accredited qualifications have been justified by fears of providers simply signing up people onto non-accredited courses, with little way of measuring progression and achievement. The fear of eternal students taking courses throughout their lives explains why the entitlements are restricted to a first full qualification.

However, the evidence shows that the current system leads to similar problems. Many people are on accredited courses that are not right for them, and a high proportion fail to achieve their qualifications. The achievement rate for NVQs is notoriously low – 53 per cent at level 2 in 2003/04 (LSC benchmarking data). This is largely because learners and employers alike have more enthusiasm about acquiring new skills than about gaining new qualifications. This means that the advantages of the current, restricted, system have been exaggerated, and that there would be few risks for the learners in giving them more flexible options. A well-defined new entitlement would give more choice to learners, while still circumscribing the amount of provision that they could access.

A new flexible entitlement for those without a level 2 qualification

The new flexible entitlement would be based on need rather than on the type of provision or on whether it is full or part time. Everyone without a level 2 qualification would be allowed free access to any type of provision up to level 2 – including at entry level, level 1 and partial level 2 – and to progress to a full level 2. As is currently the case, those without level 2 but who are able to progress immediately to level 3 should be able (and encouraged) to jump a level.

The new flexible entitlement would guarantee free tuition for the notional equivalent in guided learning hours of a two-year full-time course, in addition to the existing entitlement to a first full level 2 qualification. This would enable students to choose their own pathways, which could take a wide variety of forms.

For example, they could decide to embark on part-time courses alongside their work for several years, or could concentrate all their entitlement in two years, full time. They would be able to interrupt their studies, taking a break of several years after achieving their level 1 before going on to a level 2 course. They would also be able to start with an entry-level course, continue with a level 1 and then prepare a level 2 qualification with their existing entitlement. The option to take a qualification would thus ultimately remain, but would not constrain the types of courses that individuals could take in the first place.

In order to avoid the fraud encountered on earlier schemes, such as the Individual Learning Accounts, the entitlement would have to be taken with an LSC-accredited provider. The LSC would also make sure that the provision is appropriately inspected – particularly where it is not leading to a qualification. The individual learner records maintained through a learning account (or through a 'unique learner number', once these are developed) would allow the LSC to keep track of people's progress and check their use of the entitlement.

The new flexible entitlement would have additional costs. This is because people who are not tempted by, or able to embark on, a full level 2 qualification may be attracted to more flexible options, and might stay in learning for longer. However, many of the courses covered by the new flexible entitlement are likely to be significantly less expensive than the ones covered by the existing entitlement, as they would not need to lead to externally accredited qualifications. Significant resources could be obtained to pay for this by re-orientating funding from existing initiatives. Most importantly, substantial resources could be saved by scaling back, or even scrapping, Train to Gain.

The main problem with Train to Gain is that it defeats the very purpose that it is meant to achieve – trying to get employers to train their workforce. Rather than encouraging them to invest in training, providing employers with free training and wage compensations is more likely to encourage them to believe that all training costs should fall back on the state. The massive deadweight of up to 90 per cent that was recorded in the pilots is testimony to this.

Even though Train to Gain is now insisting more on aiming at hard-to-reach employers, it is doubtful that an employer's long-term approach to training can be changed by giving it free provision. Furthermore, the programme undermines one of the key components of learning – individual empowerment – by getting employers, rather than learners, to choose the training provided. Finally, the system needs to pay for brokers, without which hard-to-reach employers would be even less likely to become engaged. However, brokers are expensive (in 2007/08, they will represent 7.6 per cent of the total cost of the programme), diverting significant resources from where they are most needed – teaching and learning.

If we can develop a more flexible system of entitlement, then there is a very strong case for re-orientating funding of Train to Gain towards it. Some employers might lose out on the current situation, but their employees should benefit as they would be able to access provision of their choice, rather than just fitting the needs of their current job.

In 2007/08, £473 million will be devoted to Train to Gain (including £38 million for wage compensation and £36 million for brokerage). This is expected to pay for about 200,000 full level-2 starts (leading to 45,500 achievements) and about 34,500 basic skills starts (leading to 3850 achievements). This means that a total of £2020 will be paid for each new learner. This is expensive when we consider that of the average 50 hours contact time for those taking NVQs at level 2 only 17 hours consist of effective teaching, with the rest taken up with assessment and portfolio building (Hillage *et al* 2006).

In comparison, a full-time course of study at level 2 constitutes around 450–569 guided learning hours. The current basic annual rate for this is generally between £2576 and £4122, depending on the programme weighting – in other words, taking into account the fact that courses such as engineering are inherently more expensive than business studies, for example (LSC 2006c). Taking an average of £3300, this would mean that a hypothetical 143,000 people could take up full-time learning with the funds used for Train to Gain in 2007/08. Significantly more could take up courses on a part-time basis, as is possible with Train to Gain programmes.

Shifting from Train to Gain to the new flexible entitlement would benefit roughly the same number of learners, but the resources would be used for teaching and learning, rather than merely for assessing. What is more, the system would no longer be subsidising employers who would train their workforce in any case.

The best way of introducing such changes would be to test and evaluate the different programmes alongside each other. Pilots of the new flexible entitlement could be introduced in some areas in order to evaluate take-up and progression of learners starting at different levels.

An additional option would be to pilot a revised version of Train to Gain in which employees, rather than employers, decide which courses to take. Employers participating in the scheme would agree to release their employees for the time of their study. Even if employees enrolled in courses that would not directly benefit their employer, employers would still benefit because employees who get the chance to train through their workplace are more likely to stay and to improve in their jobs. Piloting the new flexible entitlement alongside a revised Train to Gain would provide useful information on the motivations and expectations of potential learners, employees and employers.

General education for adults

There is an assumption that adults who have failed to secure a level 2 or 3 qualification before they were 19 should go onto vocational courses that will prepare them for a specific job. However, these learners might benefit from the late opportunity to gain a more broadly based qualification that could enable them to go to university, among other things.

Many of those who have failed to achieve their qualifications as teenagers are disadvantaged, and these learners should be offered a second chance at 'academic' studies. However, GCSEs and A levels are unlikely to meet their needs. The shortcomings of both qualifications are widely recognised – particularly their narrowness and the fact that they do not give sufficient importance to basic skills (see Working Group on 14–19 Reform 2004).

For young adults and later returners alike, a qualification that would be equivalent to, but different from, the 'five good GCSEs or three A levels' model might be highly motivational. The US General Education Certificate provides a good example (see Box 3.2).

In England, a new 'second-chance' qualification could build on the numerous Access to Higher Education programmes. These are designed for people who do not have the necessary qualification to enter HE, in order to provide the knowledge and skills that students will require in HE. They are usually available from the age of 19 and comprise one year of full-time study, or two years part time. They comprise one of the main routes into HE for mature students and for those from disadvantaged backgrounds. These programmes are often developed by colleges, accredited by OCN and recognised by the Quality Assurance Agency for Higher Education (HEFCE 2006).

It would make sense to develop courses that build on these key characteristics of broad, general and flexible delivery adapted to the needs of learners. Such provision could also be created at level 2, as a first step towards Access provision (or A levels).

Box 3.2: The American General Educational Development Diploma

The General Educational Development Diploma (GED) is equivalent to the High School Diploma – the main end-of-school qualification in the United States that is obtained by 90 per cent of students at the age of 18. The GED was created in the 1940s to help young veterans gain access to the equivalent of a High School Diploma. Since then, it has evolved as a 'second chance', particularly for people who dropped out of school early, immigrants, members of minority ethnic groups and people who have been through the criminal justice system. The average age of GED candidates is 25 years.

The GED is awarded on completion of a series of tests in five areas: writing, social studies, science, interpreting literature and the arts, and mathematics. To pass the GED, the candidate must perform at least as well as six out of 10 high-school seniors nationwide, though individual states can set stricter requirements. Some states ask students to take an additional test showing an understanding of federal, state, and/or local government. Tutoring is often financed by the education boards of individual states, and is free of charge to students.

Research shows that in terms of the labour market, those who hold a GED are not the equivalent to those with a High School Diploma, and tend to earn less (OECD 2005b). However, this is largely due to the self-selection of individuals taking the diploma. For low-attaining individuals, the additional skills acquired during the process of preparing for the GED bring substantial rewards compared with non-GED holders with comparable (in other words, very poor) levels of attainment at high school (Jenkins and Wolf 2005). About 95 per cent of US colleges and universities consider the GED equivalent to the High School Diploma.

Improved information, advice and guidance

Giving more choice to learners means that information, advice and guidance (IAG) will become more crucial than ever. The Government has planned to revise current arrangements, and it will be important to ensure that everyone who needs it has easy access to personalised guidance. The extended learndirect telephone advice service, which has been trialled since 2006, offers in-depth guidance, and should provide an important point of entry. It is complemented by face-to-face counselling in IAG partnerships, such as nextsteps, which contracts with providers including learndirect.

However, the multiplication of brands, such as nextsteps and learndirect, has proved unhelpful, and makes it more difficult for learners to navigate the system. It would make sense to rationalise the structure. Learndirect enjoys widespread recognition, and an evaluation has shown the quality of the service provided (Page *et al* forthcoming). Learndirect centres are often located in colleges, Jobcentre Plus and community centres, and are widely accessible.

So, the learndirect advice remit (currently limited to those in need of basic skills, level 2 and level 3 provision) should be extended to all types of learners and be retained as the single national agency for IAG. As suggested by the Leitch Review, this new universal adult careers service should retain the current learndirect budget and subsume the nextsteps budget (Leitch 2006).

Conclusions

The basic skills and level 2 targets have helped draw attention to the most disadvantaged groups. However, they have often resulted in provision being reduced to a matter of getting people through the tests, with a focus on numbers rather than quality, and have failed to reach those with the greatest need. The central role given to externally accredited qualifications consumes significant resources that could be more usefully spent on improving adults' learning experience and ensuring that they build up their skills.

The system needs to engage learners by offering them more choice in the type of provision that they are entitled to, and making more flexible and personalised provision available, including a general, non-vocational, option. In order to give people access to a wider range of provision, financial support needs to be improved, and this is the focus of the next chapter.

4. Funding, fees and financial support

Since 2003, the Government's funding and fees policy has been increasingly realigned according to the priorities spelt out in its skills strategy. Those studying towards basic skills, a first full level 2 or, in some cases, level 3 qualification, have access to free tuition. Adults wanting to access other courses have to pay an increasing proportion of the costs, which within a few years will rise to 50 per cent. Unlike in Higher Education, they have to pay for them upfront before starting their course.

Fees and funding policies have the potential to improve redistribution of opportunities in favour of disadvantaged groups, and there is a strong case for raising fees if this allows better targeting on those who need it most. However, the recent changes have taken place in the context of a reduced rate of growth of the further education budget, and this suggests that the Government is unlikely to liberate any new funds. As a result, some adults are being left out of the equation, or are not receiving free access to the type of provision that would suit them most, and financial support has not yet been adapted to respond to the needs of adult learners who have to pay increasing fees.

The current system lacks coherence, and is not always skewed towards those who need it most. The objectives for funding and financial support should be twofold. First, public policy needs to make sure that viable provision can be accessed by all, at a reasonable cost, with financial support available at rates close to commercial rates for everyone who would like to access further learning. Second, higher levels of financial support need to be available to those who are more disadvantaged.

Government policy on subsidies and fees

The Government has advanced two reasons for its changes in policy on funding and fees: a decision to redirect funding towards priority provision, and a desire to improve the provider base, as it was feared that low direct incomes would prevent providers from delivering high-quality courses (DfES *et al* 2003). The decision was described as being in accordance with principles of public service reform, to make learning providers more sustainable and less dependent on government subsidy, and to create a real market.

Box 4.1 explains the three key concepts of LSC funding: fee subsidies, fee remissions and the fee assumption. Fee subsidies and fee remissions are important, because the support offered to learners through paying for the direct costs of provision is the largest single element of support. The advantage of fee subsidies is that learners can immediately and clearly see whether they have access to free or low-cost provision. However, they lack differentiation, so they often support learners who could afford to pay, and they require learners to be matched to subsidised provision, rather than responding more directly to learners' needs.

Box 4.1: Fee subsidy, fee assumption and fee remission

Further education courses are financed by the LSC. Each provider receives an allocation of funds based on anticipated enrolments. Learners entitled to free provision – those studying towards their first basic skills, full level 2 or, in some cases, level 3 qualification and those dependent on income-related benefits – are fully subsidised by the LSC (the *fee subsidy*). For other students, the funding assumes that the fee subsidy paid by the LSC will be complemented by an individual fee. This is called the *fee assumption.*

Colleges are not obliged to charge fees, and commonly offer fee *remissions* on top of the LSC categories. Fee remissions can be full, giving learners totally free courses, or partial. Fee remissions are at the discretion of colleges, which typically grant them to low-income applicants or particular types of courses (Perry and Fletcher 2006).

New policy on funding and fees

The overall fee assumption is the level of course fees that providers are expected to collect from individuals and employers. Some providers may choose not to collect these fees, or to vary their level. The LSC raised the fee assumption from 25 per cent to 27.5 per cent for 2005/06 and by a further five percentage points in the two following years, taking the contribution from individuals or employers up to 32.5 per cent and then 37.5 per cent in 2007/08 (LSC 2005a). Its fee assumption is expected to rise further over time, to 50 per cent.

This marks a significant shift from the policy that Labour set out in its first term. The objective of 'widening participation' meant that incentives were given to increase FE student numbers. Learning providers were encouraged to increase enrolments, particularly on short courses, almost regardless of the subject area or level of the programme of study, although curbs on government subsidy of non-accredited learning were set quite early on.

As a result, many colleges ended up collecting no fees at all on a whole range of courses. Survey evidence suggests that in 2002/03, 56 per cent of all courses on offer attracted either full or partial remission through a combination of national policy and college discretion (Challis and Pye 2003). The number of learners granted remission under college discretion was almost double that qualifying within the LSC categories, such as the national entitlements and people receiving benefits. The LSC now expects colleges to revise their fee policies in order to become more aligned with these national priorities, and colleges are increasingly discouraged from remitting fees for non-priority learners.

Fee policy and redistribution

There are very good reasons for wanting changes in fee policy, as the blanket fee remissions and subsidies applied from the late 1990s onwards have not always worked in favour of those who needed them most.

Figure 4.1 shows a breakdown of fee subsidy for learners on full-time courses, according to the Mosaic[2] social groups of beneficiaries. These groups are ranked according to their income levels, and although the postcode analysis used remains somewhat crude, the pattern is clear, and shows that in 2004/05, a significant proportion of fee subsidy went to people living in areas characterised as being relatively affluent (categories A to C). This suggests that many of these beneficiaries could probably have afforded to pay for their courses, and there is a strong case for redistributing this form of support.

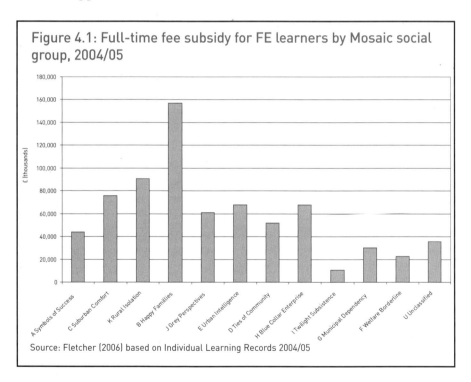

Figure 4.1: Full-time fee subsidy for FE learners by Mosaic social group, 2004/05

Source: Fletcher (2006) based on Individual Learning Records 2004/05

---

2. Mosaic provides a population classification of citizens at postcode and household level on the basis of a range of factors including their economic, social, and demographic characteristics, and a wide range of health, education, and criminal justice indicators.

When colleges use their discretion to remit fees, they currently forego up to 32.5 per cent of the estimated income attributable to that course. They can often make up this shortfall in income by using part-time staff, franchising courses and delivering programmes at a lower cost (Challis and Pye 2003), but this is likely to impact on the quality of provision.

There is an overall consensus on the need to review fee policy, albeit with important caveats concerning the extent of fee increases. Surveys show that overall rebalancing of the contribution of the state, employers and individuals is considered necessary, including by college leaders (MORI Social Research Institute 2005, Perry and Fletcher 2006). In a survey for NIACE in 2006, a representative sample of the population indicated their belief that individual learners should pay for most of their courses, ranging from 40 per cent of the total cost for those on basic skills and level 2 programmes to more than 80 per cent of personal development courses (Aldridge and Tuckett 2006b).

The impact of rising fees

Most colleges reported a drop in their recruitment of adult students in 2005–06. This depletion is partly due to the fact that colleges have had to reduce their course offers as a result of reduced funding from the LSC. It is also due to their need to re-focus on fewer, longer, courses that meet targets (Perry and Fletcher 2006). However, there are some fears that a fee-driven college might attract a different client base, and that some might decide to leave outreach work to local authorities or other agencies.

Further fee rises are likely to affect full-time adult courses, including Access courses, though many colleges have retained concessions for learners within this category (Perry and Fletcher 2006). Personal, community and development learning (PCDL) is being sidelined, but no coherent system has been set up to ensure adequate provision. It has been left up to local authorities to step in to make up for the loss of LSC funding, but there is no guarantee that they will do so, nor that all disadvantaged adults will be able to access this type of provision. A transition phase should be put in place with clearer roles and responsibilities for the LSC and local authorities – an issue that will be further explored in the final chapter of this report.

The actual and expected impacts of fee rises suggest that further developments will require close monitoring in order to ensure that the needs of those with lesser means to pay continue to be addressed. Evidence should be collected on the impact that changes have on different social groups, as suggested by the House of Commons Education and Skills Committee (2006).

Financial support for adult learners

The introduction of tuition fees in higher education in 2006 was expected to provide additional resources that would improve provision and would subsidise bursaries for poorer students. In contrast, in FE, fees are being increased alongside cuts in provision. Additionally, no significant steps have been taken to improve financial support for those hit by the changes, except for the new entitlement to free tuition for a first full level 3 qualification, but only for those aged up to 25.

It makes sense to put in place a viable learning offer that is not entirely dependent on the state. Changes in fee policy potentially offer a good opportunity for redistribution, but further steps need to be taken to ensure that everyone has a fair chance of accessing learning. The system of financial support plays a crucial role in targeting help towards those who cannot afford to learn. Table 4.1 (next page) describes the different forms of government-funded financial support that are available. These can be divided into four different categories, according to the types of costs that they are expected to cover, as follows:

- direct costs
- indirect costs
- living costs
- wage compensation.

These are explained in more detail below.

Category 1: Direct costs – fee remissions and fee subsidies
The direct costs of learning – in other words, tuition fees – are usually paid for through the provision of learning opportunities at no charge, or at substantially discounted rates. As seen in the previous chapter, these are mainly offered as national entitlements and fee remissions for courses at specific levels – basic skills, level 2 or (in some cases) 3 – or in skill shortage areas. Specific categories of adults are also targeted, such as those in receipt of means-tested social security benefits or, for example, mothers preparing to return to the labour market. But there is an expectation that these beneficiaries will go on to priority courses as well.

As seen earlier, colleges have had widely varying practices with regard to fee remissions. Most use them to complement the Government's approach, based on course levels, with a means-tested approach, where they help those students who fall outside the national entitlements but are nevertheless on low incomes.

Category 2: Indirect costs – one-off payments
The extra indirect costs of studying, such as transport, books or childcare, are mainly paid for through Learner Support Funds (LSF), which can also be used for tuition fees. These are significantly more targeted than fee subsidies, and are usually means tested. In 2003/04, the total expenditure on

Table 4.1: Government-funded financial support for adult learners

Costs	Financial measure	Recipients	Course restrictions
Direct costs	National entitlements to free tuition	Leaners without basic skills	Accredited basic skills courses
		Learners without a level 2 qualification	First full level 2 (or in some cases, level 3) qualification
		Learners up to age 25 without level 3 qualification	First full level 3 qualification
		All	Level 3 qualification in technical and associate professional skills in skill shortage areas
		Adults re-skilling for new careers or preparing to return to labour market	Skill shortage areas
		Learners in receipt of means-tested social security benefits	Primarily LSC priorities
	Fee subsidy by LSC: overall 75% in 2004/05 to 50% in medium term	Remaining categories of adults	At discretion of college, with regard to LSC priorities
	Discretionary fee remissions by colleges	Remaining categories of adults	At discretion of college, with regard to LSC priorities
Indirect costs	Learner Support Funds	For adults at risk of not participating or completing, one-off and urgent costs (usually means-tested): • financial hardship and emergencies • childcare costs • accommodation costs, for those who have to study beyond daily travelling distance (resid'l bursary) • tuition, registration and exam fees • travel costs • essential course-related equipment, materials and field trips	At discretion of college, with regard to LSC priorities
Living costs	Adult Learning Grant: weekly payment of up to £30 a week	Income below £19,000 (individual) or £30,000 (household). To be rolled out nationally from 2007/8. Conditional on satisfactory weekly course attendance.	Full-time study for a first level 2 or 3 qualification. Normally paid for up to two years, or up to three years if immediate progression to a first full level 3
	Career Development Loans: £300–£8,000. Available through an arrangement between LSC and banks at a fixed rate	People unable to pay for the following costs themselves: • course fees (100% of course fees when out of	*cont. next page*

Living	Financial measure	Recipients	Course restrictions
costs (cont.)	of interest. Loan interest paid while studying.	work for three months or more, otherwise 80%) • other course costs (e.g. equipment, childcare, travel) • living expenses	Up to two years, vocational (work-related) learning, or up to 3 years if this includes one year of relevant practical work experience. Excludes foundation courses used as first step towards a degree course
	Residential Bursary Funds	Students in specialist colleges beyond daily travelling distance (means tested)	Agricultural, horticultural and art and design specialisms
	Dance and Drama Awards	For students in specialist schools (means tested)	Dance and drama
Wage compen-sation	Child Benefit Child Tax Credit (plus the related passported benefits)	Parents or carers of 19- to 20-year-olds who are still learning up to level 3, when they enrol before 19	
	Incapacity Benefit	People who are unable to work because of illness or disability	
	Income Support	People on low income who are unemployed (or work on average fewer than 16 hours a week)	
	Jobseeker's Allowance	Unemployed people not in full-time education (or who work on average fewer than 16 hours a week)	
	Payment of £10 per week for basic skills training, with an additional £100 for achievement of a qualification	For Jobseeker's Allowance recipients with literacy, language and/or numeracy below level 1	Literacy, language or numeracy training leading towards a recognised qualification
	Train to Gain wage costs scheme: £5 per hour or actual wage for every hour	Employers with fewer than 50 employees	First full level 2 or basic skills qualification

LSF for learners over 19 was £96.5 million, for a total of 200,000 learners, including £34 million ringfenced for childcare support.

The LSF is allocated to colleges on the basis of local levels of deprivation and the profile of students. It is then managed and distributed to students at the level of the FE institution, within set national guidelines that define high priority groups (for example, people on benefits or low income, lone parents, disabled students and basic skills students). Local priorities can also be identified and set at an institutional level.

As a system that balances local discretion with national recommendations, the LSF seems to work well. It is considered straightforward to admin-
ister and flexible in the support it offers. Evaluations suggest that the LSF is
effective in targeting those with the greatest financial needs, and this is
reflected in the social and demographic profile of fund recipients (Tyers and
Bates 2005). LSF recipients are more likely to stay on, and are as likely to
achieve as non-supported learners. This is a positive outcome considering
the fact that they tend to be more disadvantaged (Dewson *et al* 2003).

Category 3: Living costs – grants and loans
While they are engaged in learning, students have a reduced capacity to pay
for their living costs. Apart from Residential Bursary Funds and Dance and
Drama Awards (which cater for highly specialised students), the main
forms of support comes in the form of Adult Learning Grants (ALGs) and
Career Development Loans (CDLs).

The ALG is a means-tested grant to adults studying full time for a first
full level 2 or 3 qualification. As it only provides a maximum of £30 a week,
it cannot appropriately cover the living costs of independent students, and
is closer to the Educational Maintenance Allowance, which is available as an
incentive for 16- to 19-year-olds to stay on. Unsurprisingly, evaluations of
the pilots showed that this grant was mainly taken up by people aged under
22 who were still living with their parents (70 per cent of recipients)
(Michaelson *et al* 2005).

CDLs can cover living costs, as well as direct and indirect costs. Eligibility
is based on course type and the ability to repay. This explains why successful CDL applicants are not typical of the population of working age, and
tend to be young, well educated and well qualified – 41 per cent were graduates, according to an evaluation carried out in 2000 (Wells and Murphy
2001). Many recipients also go on to high-level study – 30 per cent were for
postgraduate qualifications, 10 per cent for first degrees and 34 per cent for
specific vocational qualifications. The deadweight was estimated at around
55 per cent.

Given these characteristics, CDLs only support a small minority of students in further education, and do not appear to provide adequate support
for those on lower-level courses who are more disadvantaged (17,000 new
learners in 2003/04, with a budget of £14.8m, supporting a total loan allocation by the banks of £73.9m). For those who use them, they are considered relatively safe and cheap – the average default rate across all users in a
five-year period from 1995 to 2000 was under 10 per cent (Stuart 2001).

Category 4: Wage compensation – benefits
Although benefits are not directly linked to learning (except for Child

Benefit and Child Tax Credits extensions), they do support many learners *de facto*, as indicated by Figure 4.2, which shows the proportions of learners receiving the different kinds of financial support.

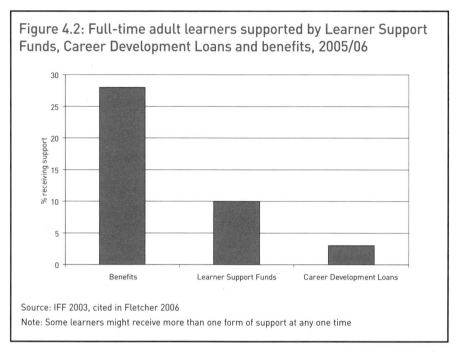

Figure 4.2: Full-time adult learners supported by Learner Support Funds, Career Development Loans and benefits, 2005/06

Source: IFF 2003, cited in Fletcher 2006
Note: Some learners might receive more than one form of support at any one time

A survey carried out in 2005 showed that 14 per cent of people on Jobseeker's Allowance (JSA), 7 per cent on Incapacity Benefit and 10 per cent on Income Support were currently studying on some type of taught course – not necessarily related to employability (Prior *et al* 2006). However, within the UK the overall approach towards the unemployed remains resolutely based on a 'work first' principle, with the priority being to get people back into work as quickly as possible. This explains why JSA and Income Support regulations do not allow recipients to study for more than 16 hours per week.

Similarly, 'welfare to work' policies put very little emphasis on education and training. The various forms of New Deal include a full-time education option, which covers the costs of fees, books, travel or equipment, but this remains relatively marginal: 18- to 24-year-olds can normally only access it after six months' continuous claim to JSA, rising to 18 months for those over 25. Disabled people and lone parents receive some support in arranging training, and some help with related expenses. The latest welfare White Paper, *A New Deal for Welfare* (DWP 2006), focuses on 'harder to reach' groups – those on incapacity benefits and long-term unemployment or economic inactivity – but education and skills remain marginal to the strategy.

Nevertheless, there have been some attempts at a different approach. The literacy and numeracy needs of claimants are now screened within six months of claiming, and those below level 1 can access free tuition. Incentives to attend this tuition now come in the form of a £10 payment per week, with an additional £100 for those who achieve a qualification. The Work-Based Learning for Adults programme also offers a different approach, in the form of short-term or longer-term work experience and job-focused training, to those aged 25 and over who have been out of work for six months or more. Evaluation of this programme has revealed significant positive employment-related outcomes for some participants (Speckesser and Bewley 2006).

Finally, a New Deal for Skills, launched in 2005, comprises 'skills coaching' by Jobcentre Plus personal advisers, 'skills passports' to record individual skills and, since 2006, trials for a 'learning option' to test the effectiveness of a small financial incentive to encourage low-skilled Jobcentre Plus customers to take up full-time level 2 courses (DfES *et al* 2005). It is still too early to say whether these initiatives may signal a change in approach.

A learner-led system

The current system of fee subsidies and financial support for learners does not amount to a coherent system – it is not sufficiently redistributive. Furthermore, the increasing focus on government priorities means that the needs of several categories of learners are not appropriately met – in particular, part-time students, those on low income who already have a level 2 qualification, and those without a level 2 but who may need other types of provision.

What is required is a system that matches the diverse needs of learners, rather than only supporting those whose characteristics match the priorities defined according to the needs of the economy. This means that more flexible support should be available to priority groups, with appropriate financing options for other groups.

New Learning Accounts

The Government has decided to launch a new version of Learning Accounts, to be trialled from autumn 2007 (DfES 2006b). The Leitch Review of Skills recommended that all adult vocational further education funding for individuals in England, including the current level 2 entitlement, be channelled through Learner Accounts by 2010 (Leitch 2006). However, how these will work in practice remained undefined at the time of writing. They are likely to share many characteristics with the previous generation of Individual Learning Accounts, described in Box 4.2.

It is as yet unclear what the added value of the new Learning Accounts

Box 4.2: From Individual Learning Accounts to the new Learning Accounts

The Learning Accounts, in both guises, are virtual funds that learners can use to buy courses at their own discretion. They are administered by a third party. Contributions are expected from the state, employers and individuals. When Individual Learning Accounts (ILAs) were launched in 2000, a £150 incentive was offered to the first one million account holders, on the condition that they contributed at least £25. Employers did not have to pay tax or National Insurance on their contribution, as long as the facility was extended to the lowest paid employers in the company. In practice, few employers contributed over the life of the ILAs (Gray *et al* 2002).

ILAs provided differential discounts: 20 per cent (up to a maximum of £100) on the individual's cost of a broad range of learning, and 80 per cent (up to a maximum of £200) on a limited list of IT, literacy and numeracy courses. There were restrictions on the types of courses that could be accessed – for example, the scheme excluded leisure and sports activities, and graduate and postgraduate courses.

In terms of numbers, ILAs appeared successful – 690,000 individuals had opened an account after six months of operation (Gray *et al* 2002). However, many of them had already decided to start their courses before even hearing about ILAs, and the deadweight was estimated at about 54 per cent (Owens 2001, 2002). The vast majority of learners participating in the scheme already possessed some form of qualification (82 per cent), and 36 per cent had a qualification at level 4 or above. Thus their effect in attracting new learners appears to have been limited.

Unlike the ILAs, the new Learning Accounts can only be used with LSC-accredited providers, in order to avoid the fraud that led to the curtailment of ILAs after only one year in operation. Another major difference is that while ILAs were available to all adults, the new Learning Accounts will be tested with those studying for a level 3 qualification, on the basis that they are 'able and motivated to exercise real choice' (DfES 2006b).

will be. As the ILA experience shows, when learners only hear about the accounts through the learning providers that they have already contacted, the accounts act as little more than a form of fee remission. The initial concept of the accounts was to give future learners and their employers real incentives to save and 'invest' in their account. However, unless putting money in the account results in real benefits, the policy simply adds extra administrative burden for providers and complexity for learners. Indeed, it is unclear why learners should have more incentive to pay for learning through an account than they would have when they pay their partly remitted fees, beyond the symbolic value of 'holding' an account – particularly if (as seems likely) the accounts are virtual.

An alternative to these Learning Accounts would be a new flexible entitlement for those without a level 2 qualification, as suggested in the previous chapter, coupled with flexible support for indirect costs, grants and income-contingent loans for those who need support for living costs.

Flexible financial support

Free tuition may not be sufficient to enable some people to take up learning. Financial support should be available to those for whom the Adult Learning Grant is inappropriate, either because the sum is too small, or because they are not on a first full-time level 2 or 3 course.

Discretionary funding appears to be the most appropriate way of supporting people who are unable to pay for indirect or one-off costs. It has proved its worth, and a discretionary approach offers the flexibility to adapt funding to the highly individualised needs of specific learners, as well as making the best use of resources at the local level. Discretionary funding is currently offered by colleges through their discretionary fee remissions, and by Learner Support Funds. The Leitch Review recommended replacing them with Skills Development Funds, which would not be offered through colleges, but at the discretion of the new Careers Services (Leitch 2006).

The advantage of discretionary funding is that clear criteria could be defined for each area, and these could then be publicised, thus raising awareness of support entitlements among disadvantaged potential learners before they considered taking up learning. However, this system could only work if the new Career Services become sufficiently established. The (as yet undefined) eligibility criteria would have to remain sufficiently flexible to allow for a wide variety of individual cases. Meanwhile, college and Career Service advisers would need to retain a degree of discretion, and would be held accountable for using funds on the basis of student need – as defined by income and educational attainment.

Students may also need support with living costs. Adults who take level 3 and 4 courses in the learning and skills sector should be given access to income-contingent loans (addressed in the following subsection), as they have good prospects of earning a healthy income. However, for most of those studying at level 2 and below this is unlikely to be the method of choice, as the returns to these qualifications are low, and these students are – understandably – the most averse to debt (Callender 2006).

Most of those studying at or below level 2 are likely either to learn part time while in full-time or part-time employment, or to receive benefits that support their living costs. As described earlier, many are also relatively young and still live with their parents. The main gap comprises the few learners who would like to study full time while not receiving any benefits.

The best approach here is likely to be a flexible one that enables colleges to extend their discretionary Learner Support Funds in order to help towards living costs. Local grant systems could also be devised, with the criteria to allocate grants set by local government.

Income-contingent loans

Career Development Loans do not provide sufficiently extensive or broad support for those studying at higher levels. The Leitch Review suggested improving these loans by raising the cap on the public funds available to pay for interest and as guarantee, so that more people could access the loans (Leitch 2006). However, this does not go far enough.

Even after the introduction in 2006 of £3,000 top-up fees for university students, the UK funding system remains significantly more favourable to HE, rather than FE, students. The introduction of income-contingent loans on the same basis that they are available in HE would go some way to redressing this imbalance.

The advantage of income-contingent loans, particularly when compared to Career Development Loans, is that some of the risk is borne by the state, rather than the individual, if the learning does not pay off. It also means that prospective learners do not have to meet a commercial bank's criteria of being 'loan-worthy', and this enables more people to take up the opportunity.

In HE, students taking loans are currently at an advantage not only because of income contingency, which means that they only have to repay after they have reached the income threshold, but also because they pay zero interest rates. This system is regressive, as it subsidises all students in HE irrespective of their ability to pay, while those in FE are subject to commercial interest rates. The Government should reconsider this issue when it revises the funding settlement in HE in 2009.

Ideally, market interest rates should apply post-graduation, with zero real rates during the period of study (Piatt and Robinson 2001). Applying such a system across the HE and FE sectors would ensure that all students would benefit, wherever they studied, and would free up more resources to support the most disadvantaged with grants and free provision. Other options to be considered are interest subsidies on a sliding scale, with lower interest rates for those on level 3 courses or for those training towards specific occupations, such as nursing.

In the meantime, FE students should be entitled to the same income-contingent and interest-free loans as those available to HE students. Like HE students, students in FE should be allowed to finance any course, including foundation courses used as first steps towards a degree course, through their loans – and should not be restricted to vocational courses.

Supporting welfare benefit recipients

Acquiring new skills and engaging with other learners may be an excellent use of time for those who are unemployed. The Government has adopted a 'job-first' approach in which the priority is to get the unemployed back into work. This is very different from the approach adopted in other European countries, where skills improvement is an inherent part of any unemployment strategy. However, there are a few practical ways in which access to learning could be facilitated for those who are receiving benefits – for example:

- **Scrapping the 16-hour study rule** For those in receipt of Jobseeker's Allowance, the definition of full-time study at 16 hours is too restrictive, and goes against the logic of improving a person's skills over what should hopefully remain a short period of forced inactivity. The 16-hour rule should be scrapped, but the person would still have to comply with job-searching requirements and to take a job when they find one. It would still be necessary to distinguish between full-time students and unemployed people who are studying while searching for a job, as the former would not be entitled to unemployment benefits.

- **Enabling individuals to complete courses in their own time** It should be made easier for unemployed people who find a job while they are on a course to finish the course and achieve their qualification in their own time. This is often hampered by the fact that Jobcentre Plus provision usually takes place during the day. Systems should be in place to ensure that these learners can be transferred onto courses that take place at suitable times so that they can gain more from their involvement in learning. Closer collaboration between the LSC and Jobcentre Plus appears crucial in order to achieve this – an issue that will be further explored in Chapter 5.

- **Providing early information, advice and guidance on learning opportunities** Recipients of welfare benefits should be directed towards information, advice and guidance (IAG) at an early stage, to make sure they start considering learning or self-improvement options, even if self-financed, from the start. The Leitch Review suggested that all individuals be screened for basic skills needs at the start of their claim, rather than after six months of unemployment (Leitch 2006). This is an important step. Going further, Jobcentre Plus should ensure that all clients without qualifications are referred to the Careers Service, and that all those without a level 2 are given the opportunity to take advantage of the service and of skills training.

Conclusions

The Government's new funding and fee policy has the potential to improve redistribution of opportunities in favour of disadvantaged groups. However, financial support has not yet adapted to the dual needs of the priority groups and of those who have to pay increasing fees. A more coherent system needs to take account of how people can pay for their learning and to scale support according to their needs, rather than the supposed economic usefulness of the qualification that they pursue.

For those who benefit from an entitlement, college discretionary funds should be used to support part of the indirect costs of learning, with a requirement to target those on low incomes and the highest level of needs. For those studying at higher levels, income-contingent loans should be introduced. Students in the learning and skills sector should increasingly be treated in the same way as those in HE, in advance of the 2009 review of financial support in HE.

5. An institutional framework for adult learning

Since 2001, when the Learning and Skills Council was created as a funding body enhanced with strong planning powers, the Government has shifted its emphasis towards market mechanisms. Adult learning providers are expected to operate in a market in which consumer choice drives the learning offer, and competition ensures that prices are kept down while quality remains high.

However, this theory is not entirely realised in practice. Adult learning is much more akin to a mixed economy, where providers are heavily influenced by LSC funding and targets and only compete on specific aspects of their provision. It is often the case that a drive to create a market leads to increasing attempts to regulate it, as the Government wants to ensure that its resources are used in the way it favours.

Combining market principles with the planning function may be unhelpful in trying to reform the institutional framework for adult learning. In order for the system to be responsive to the demands of its users, more devolution is required, both to frontline providers and to local government. The system of national entitlements should ensure that basic minimum provision is available to all, with learner choice being the key principle driving the system.

Towards an adult learning 'market'?

The Foster Review of Further Education (Foster 2005) presented a relatively balanced approach to reform. The review was sympathetic to colleges, and was wary of suggesting yet another overhaul for a sector that is already in a state of perpetual reform.

Some of the more innovative proposals included progressively introducing self-regulation (involving peer assessment) as a way of improving quality. However, it was mainly its more cautious proposals – particularly around the mission, contestability and specialisation of colleges – that were taken further by the subsequent FE White Paper, *Further Education: Raising skills, improving life chances* (DfES 2006b). Nevertheless, the main reasons for Foster's caution remain valid, and may explain the vagueness of some of the proposals set out in the White Paper.

The White Paper was published in the midst of a significant government push for bolder public service reform, and probably reflects this broader context more than the specific needs of the learning and skills sector. Since New Labour's second term in office, the main themes of public service reform have been:

- choice for consumers – both in principle, and as a way of driving competition between providers
- competition and specialisation – which are expected to increase the efficiency and quality of service
- collaboration – which is promoted in order to mitigate any negative effects of competition.

Mission and specialisation

One of the necessary steps towards creating a market, according to the Government, is to have more diverse institutions responding to the diverse needs of their users. The FE White Paper seeks to focus the mission of the FE system more clearly on skills and attributes needed for employment. This could potentially be relatively disruptive for general FE colleges, which offer a wide range of provision, but its definition of 'employability' is so broad that it includes general education that could improve the soft skills valued by employers.

As noted by the House of Commons Education and Skills Committee (2006), the Government needs to spell out more clearly what a mission focused on 'skills and employability' means if it is to guide providers in deciding what provision to offer.

The main effect of this redefinition of colleges' mission for adult learning is to exclude both general ('academic') provision and personal, community and development learning (PCDL) from general FE colleges. The White Paper expects other providers – mainly from the voluntary and community sector – to specialise in this area, with funding increasingly provided by local authorities rather than by the LSC, and fees collected from individuals.

However, there is no clear strategy to spell out how this will happen in practice. Separating PCDL from the rest of FE provision may also prove more difficult than expected, as elements within this form of learning can serve as 'first steps' provision to try to attract people back into adult learning.

The move towards specialisation mirrors what happens in specialist schools: it is seen as a way of focusing attention and improving image in what remains fundamentally a generalist institution. Centres of Vocational Excellence (CoVEs) have existed in colleges since 2001, but their impact has remained limited. The CoVE initiative has brought some additional funding to specialisms within the colleges involved, but has had limited impact on the institutions as a whole. Although retention and progression in the area of specialism have been good for short courses, this has not been the case for full-time courses at level 3, as would have been expected (ALI/Ofsted 2005). As for National Skills Academies, which have been slow to take off, their impact is likely to be quite limited beyond the walls of the institutions involved.

There are good reasons for not wanting to push specialisation any further. There is no evidence that specialist colleges perform any better than departments of general colleges offering the same subjects (Fletcher 2005). Also, specialised colleges are smaller and costlier. In fact, large FE colleges are best able to offer good value for money, by cross-subsidising more expensive subjects. Overall, federal colleges that are specialised by site offer the advantages of access to good quality equipment, with economies of scale drawn from unified administration, personnel and finance services (Perry 2005).

Choice, competition and collaboration

Giving users a choice is one of the main themes of public service reform. The FE White Paper (DfES 2006b) argues that choice should be extended – both for learners, through the new Learning Accounts, and for employers, through Train to Gain and the Sector Skills Agreements. However, as shown in previous sections, in both these cases choice is tightly constrained by the national targets. The move towards choice for learners is certainly very ambiguous, and where the demands of the state, employer and learner differ it is unclear whose preference the providers should prioritise.

Less ambiguous is the FE White Paper's drive towards increasing competition. New providers are to be encouraged to enter the market through brokers, within the Train to Gain programme. The LSC is given a formal remit to increase diversity, with competitions held as a way of bringing in new providers and allowing high performing ones to expand. Initially, competitions are expected to replace poor-quality provision. But the LSC will then go on to review provision in each area, every five years, in order to establish whether competition is needed to improve quality, promote innovation and expand provision. However, we know little about the precise impact of competition on quality, cost and – crucially, for education – on participation and attainment (Fletcher 2005).

In the model suggested by the FE White Paper, an FE college would increasingly become one among many delivery agencies that might, or might not, receive government contracts. This would be in contrast with the current role of the FE college as a public-sector institution promoting and symbolising further education that is enabled through public subsidy and cross-funding, to offer cheap and diverse provision to disadvantaged groups, among others.

The problem with simply allocating courses to the cheapest providers is that quality, stability and continuity are likely to suffer most. Also, it is unclear whether user choice would be protected, as performance-driven providers may decide to cut out the most costly and difficult provision. The existence of strong institutions that have the capacity for long-term planning is considered essential for universities and schools alike. The same should be true for institutions within the learning and skills sector.

This does not mean that there is no role for private providers, whether from the commercial or voluntary sectors. Colleges need to retain their role as strategic providers, offering a network of high-quality and dedicated centres, professional support and stability, but they need to do this within a more diverse market. This market already exists, and is the main source of training for employers, as evidenced by the fact that 28 per cent of employers who train their workforce use FE colleges (Technical Supplement to the White Paper). The fact that this is only a minority of employers should not be considered a problem, as 82 per cent of those doing this are satisfied. Meanwhile, it should not be expected that public-sector provision will replace the vast bulk of training that is privately provided (Stanton 2006).

The paradox of current government policy is that while it is attempting to impose market mechanisms on the public sector, it is simultaneously extending public funding and control over the commercial and employer-focused learning sector. For example, the FE White Paper wants to make new providers eligible for additional funding support for a limited period, where this is required, to build their capacity.

The main argument for using public resources in this way is that these providers have not benefited from years of investment that help colleges deliver provision at lower costs. However, when new enterprises enter a market, they face the same challenges, without having claim to any public funding. They are able to enter the market because they offer innovative products and services that make them attractive to customers. Many private training providers are able to build their capacity with the training allocated to them by employers, and should not be entitled to any additional funding.

The main rationale for increased competition is to get rid of 'producer capture', in which public services are run primarily for those who work in them, rather than for those who use them. Ensuring that public money is spent efficiently is clearly an essential objective, but it is not clear that imposing competition mechanisms in the FE sector has had the desired impact.

Historically, a surge in regulation tends to come after the creation of quasi-markets that increase the autonomy of institutions (Bureaucracy Review Group of Further Education and Training 2004). Administrative and back-office costs have changed little, but are now explained by the need to bid for various pots of money, to justify the detailed use of resources, and to show evidence of attainment of targets and a wide range of indicators. This may be explained by the fact that competition that is 'in the market' (in other words, aims to deliver what customers want), is different from competition 'for the market' (which aims to offer what government agencies want, on the best terms). This explains why creating a well-functioning quasi-market has remained an elusive objective.

Finally, the FE White Paper also promotes collaboration, primarily as a way of countering the negative effects that competition could have on 16–19 provision and on the choice of courses available. A few models are proposed, most of which already operate in some contexts, such as formal federations and different collaborative models to share resources with schools, other colleges and providers. However, it is unclear how institutions would be expected to collaborate further if the market becomes increasingly competitive. While collaboration and competition are not mutually exclusive, they are certainly in tension.

In summary, while strong measures do need to be in place to address poor provision, increased competition may not be the right way of tackling this issue. Expanding the market further through 'competitions' is also unlikely to bring about the expected increases in quality and cost efficiency.

Funding and planning: the role of the Learning and Skills Council

Despite the introduction of market mechanisms to the learning and skills sector, a strong planning element remains. Indeed, as noted above, the incorporation of colleges has triggered significant additional regulatory requirements. This means that colleges operate in an environment that is highly directive but also surprisingly unstable, as they constantly have to adapt to changes in national priorities, targets and funding, and respond to new initiatives (Hodgson *et al* 2005). This environment is mainly set by the Learning and Skills Council (LSC).

The creation of the LSC in 2001 had the major benefit of generating a more unified sector, and of significantly enhancing the profile of post-16 education and training in England. However, its capacity has been limited by the fact that some areas of learning – notably higher education – have remained outside its remit, and it has had to respond to the tight and sometimes conflicting framework set by PSA targets, budget constraints and DfES initiatives. Like the learning providers that it funds, the LSC has itself had to operate in a very unstable environment.

This instability has not yet come to an end. The LSC is involved in Agenda for Change – an ambitious reform process whose main aims are to move away from micro-management of providers, simplify funding and data-gathering mechanisms, and achieve a better balance between national and local priorities (LSC 2005b). The FE White Paper endorsed several of these principles, and this direction of change should be encouraged.

Achieving a balance between national and local priorities
The structure of the LSC reflects the ambition to combine national and

local objectives. This is intended to be carried out through 47 Local Learning and Skills Councils (LLSCs) backed by one central office. However, the LLSCs never managed to establish themselves in a learning and skills sector that was already complex – partly because their staff experienced some difficulties adjusting from their very different former functions in the Training and Enterprise Councils (TECs).

More fundamentally, the LLSCs remain weak intermediaries between demands from the central government and learning providers, with little influence over local allocation of funds. Today, they are mainly perceived as local agents delivering national policy (Hodgson *et al* 2005). Their lack of local legitimacy has prevented them from taking difficult decisions around the reorganisation of 16–19 provision in the strategic area reviews, and this has further undermined their credibility.

Subsequent restructurings led first to the appointment of nine new regional directors, in a structure that was meant to simplify reporting to central offices, and to be coterminous with Regional Development Agencies (RDAs), in an effort to bring together economic and skills strategies. More recently, 148 Local Partnership Teams (LPTs) have been created, to work more closely with local authorities, particularly on the 14–19 agenda. Following the abolition of the 47 sub-regional LLSCs proposed in the Further Education Bill, the LSC will currently still operate at three different levels, including the national office. This means that there are a great many intermediaries between national decision-makers and the learner.

From centralisation to micro-management

Despite its multiple organisational layers, the system remains a very centralised one, from the DfES down. Following the recommendations from the Foster Review, the FE White Paper has recognised the need to give the Department a more strategic, less operational role. Equally, the LSC is expected to stop micro-managing FE institutions, and to concentrate on ensuring that the system delivers.

In line with the proposals set out in Agenda for Change, the LSC is now expected to focus on strategic commissioning, ensuring that every area has a diverse range of high-quality post-16 providers that are able to meet the needs of all learners. Two of the Agenda for Change reforms are very positive: for the LSC to fund specific plans agreed with providers, and for year-end reconciliation of the plan, rather than of the funding, reflecting a move towards funding the capacity to deliver. These are steps in the right direction.

As noted earlier in this report, funding is increasingly aligned with strictly defined targets and performance indicators. As long as these remain the main policy tools of the system, learning providers are unlikely to feel significant increases in their autonomy. Also, the LSC purchases blocks of provision, and does not determine the particular mix of subjects. However, the system encourages providers to concentrate on the most profitable forms of provision, and this means that priority-based funding continues to strongly determine what is being offered.

It is in recognition of this issue that the Leitch Review of Skills recommends a move away from block grants to support based solely on providers' estimates of expected demand (Leitch 2006). The purpose of channelling all funding through Train to Gain and Learner Accounts is to give providers funding only as they attract customers. This proposal remains relatively undefined at the time of writing, but has the potential to create much instability for providers, with major implications for their ability to maintain their workforce, infrastructure and quality of provision.

Finally, the new competitions to be held on a five-year basis will give significant power to the LSC not only to shape the structure of provision, but also to impose its own priorities. Changes brought about in the name of the market are, in fact, likely to lead to a different form of central planning.

Sector skills planning

Alongside the LSC, the main bodies involved in planning for skills are the 25 Sector Skills Councils (SSCs). Created in 2001, the main objective of each council is to provide a forum where employers can express the skills and productivity needs of their respective sectors, in order to influence the education and training system and the use of public investment. Their main initial task has been to produce Sector Skills Agreements (SSAs) that consider the skills needed within the various sectors and the steps needed in order to provide them, such as any qualifications that should be prioritised. These agreements can then be used to help with planning.

SSAs are to act as a 'key mechanism for determining priorities for the use of public funding for adult training and skills', according to the FE White Paper. They are expected to drive LSC decisions in each region on the allocation of funds to providers.

Most of these agreements are still at a preparatory stage. However, a few problems have already arisen. First, SSCs remain government-funded bodies, driven by a government-defined agenda; rather than employer initiatives, and have had difficulties getting all – or even just the most important – employers in their sectors to commit to their plans. In this sense, they cannot claim to be truly representative of employers. An added problem is that SSCs often cover very wide sectors that bring together a whole range of employers that often have little in common, and may have very different skills requirements. As a result, many local employers do not have the resources or the interest to engage in longer-term planning for the wider sector to which they have been allocated.

Finally, the purpose of SSAs is to try to forecast the future skill needs of their sectors, so the implication is that through the planning process, learning providers would make adequate courses and places available to them. However, there is no guarantee that learners will effectively turn up to these courses, and in this case, it is the colleges, rather than the SSCs, who are expected to bear the costs.

In conclusion, it appears that giving more voice to employers has added another layer of complexity to the planning process, with the LSC, SSCs and RDAs all trying to plan skills. The main result has been reduced autonomy for the learning providers themselves. Also, when there is conflict between the objectives of the various bodies involved, it is unclear whose interests should prevail. For example, there could be tension between the LSC's basic skills and level 2 targets and the objectives of the RDAs and SSCs, which might be keen to promote level 3 provision within their sectors.

Towards devolution and horizontal integration

It is difficult to show that the introduction of further quasi-market mechanisms in the learning and skills sector would have a beneficial impact on the ultimate goals of the system: learner participation, attainment and progression. The same is true of the Leitch Review's recommendations (Leitch 2006), which could create significant instability in the system to the detriment of the quality of the learning experience.

At the same time, what is required is more choice for learners, not more planning. Frontline providers and local government are best able to identify and respond to demand. They need sufficient autonomy to adapt provision to this demand, and to be held accountable for it. Horizontal integration, which should ensure that there are better links with employment, economic regeneration and other educational phases, will also be easier at a local level.

More devolution to frontline providers

In line with earlier recommendations for more flexible entitlements, policy and funding should be less prescriptive about how colleges respond to national targets and the contribution that different localities make to overall volumes of learning outcomes. Essentially, this means slimming down planning requirements, to produce a system that is very similar to the one in Scotland.

What is required is a mature provider base – which in many cases already exists – with the flexibility to respond to the needs of its customers. Like universities, colleges need to be strategic players themselves, responsible for establishing their own institutional character and direction, rather than simply delivering plans determined by other agencies (LSDA 2005). They should come to be seen as strong public service institutions that exist alongside, and in many ways complement, private provision.

Having stable, well-recognised focal points for learning should also help in terms of outreach work. Indeed, rather than national campaigns, the best means of attracting the more disadvantaged groups are often college advertisements for courses available locally.

This model would have major implications for the funding and accountability system. Providers need the financial stability that will enable them to maintain and/or reinforce their capacity, in terms of buildings, equipment and staff training. This means that they should be able to set their own plans for the types of provision that they want to offer, rather than having provision imposed on them by other bodies. Indeed, this was suggested by the Leitch Review. However, the further, still very undefined, recommendation by the Leitch Review to move entirely away from block grants, and only to fund providers according to enrolment and achievement, is a step too far, as this would make it very difficult for providers to ensure financial stability.

Colleges need to be able to set priorities that respond to the communities they serve and to devise medium-term and long-term plans. These would be agreed with the funding body, which would then 'buy' the plan and use the standard public-sector model of auditing, to ensure that funds were spent for appropriate purposes (Bureaucracy Review Group of Further Education and Training 2004). Agenda for Change introduced three-year plans, which have rarely been applied in practice due to constant changes of requirements and procedures, but should become the norm, within a more stable funding regime.

Within this model, two main quality assurance mechanisms would be needed – monitoring and inspection, as follows:

- **Monitoring** The funding body needs to monitor provider performance against the agreed contract. Providers would be held accountable, after the event, for the way they have spent their money against the plan. The process of negotiating contracts should include an agreement on key indicators, such as participation, retention and success of priority groups. These would reflect, but would not be restricted to, the national targets. Being generated bottom up, rather than imposed from the top, they would be more adapted to local needs and would be perceived as developmental and motivational, rather than punitive.
- **Inspection** The main other quality assurance mechanism would be inspection, to assess the most important aspect of education: the quality of teaching and learning. The lighter-touch inspection model that was recently introduced is a move in the right direction.

    From 2007, the new, single inspectorate needs to make sure that it integrates the positive lessons learnt from the practice of the Adult Learning Inspectorate. This involves a dialogue with providers, to help them identify weak areas and support them to improve. Poorly performing colleges should receive more substantial help, with teams of inspectors and expert practitioners working inside institutions alongside managers and practitioners (Lucas 2005). It is on this basis that the LSC should build stronger powers of intervention to tackle failing and mediocre provision, as introduced in the Further Education Bill.

More devolution to local government

National targets and centralised course prescription have proved insufficiently sensitive to local circumstances and the needs of end users. To address this, management of learning provision should be devolved more closely to local and democratic levels of governance.

It is widely recognised that the considerable degree of centralisation in Britain, compared with that of other developed countries, has not allowed local communities – particularly within cities – to respond adequately to the economic and social challenges that they face. There is substantial evidence that economic performance at a local or city level is linked to the devolution of government functions (Marshall and Finch 2006).

To date, no such evidence has been compiled in relation to the delivery of learning and skills, because of difficulties in isolating the relevant variables. But it is significant that in most countries, these functions are indeed devolved to the local level. Devolution to local level would ensure clearer, democratic accountability for the scope and quality of provision in an area, and would make sure that there are appropriate mechanisms for the local population to influence them.

However, devolution of learning and skills cannot be considered in isolation: it needs to be linked to wider changes affecting local government. Due to the failure of the 2004 referendum for a Regional Assembly for the North East, regional governance is now a distant prospect. This is compounded by the fact that Regional Development Agencies (RDAs), which were expected to act as a catalyst of economic development, have failed to impress.

Conversely, local authorities have the significant advantage of having democratic legitimacy. In recent years they have received more powers in relation to schools and the Every Child Matters agenda. As noted in the Local Government White Paper:

'Local authorities and other partners working in collaboration in cities could have a key role in shaping a package of skills training that is strongly focused on what employers and individuals really need, ensuring that the supply of skills matches the demands of the local economy.' (DCLG 2006a: 83)

The main issue that is usually raised with regard to local authorities taking this role is that they are often too geographically small. This problem would be offset if the concept of 'city regions' (which map onto flows of economic activity beyond administrative metropolitan boundaries) gained ground. Again, the Local Government White Paper suggests that this is likely to take place, with democratic accountability ensured by the election of a leader, such as a mayor or councillor. Thus, the best option for local devolution of learning and skills functions would be a combination of city regions, where they exist, and local authorities.

The agreement reached in the only existing city region – London – offers a useful model that should be replicated elsewhere, as recommended by the Local Government White Paper. The London Mayor chairs a new London Skills and Employment Board, and will set priorities and overall direction for the delivery of adult skills in the capital (DCLG 2006b). The new single LSC for London will be required to spend its budget according to these priorities.

Progressively, we should evolve towards 'dual key' arrangements that would give city-regional authorities or local authorities and the national LSC joint control over the post-19 skills budget for the city region. This combination of national and local control would ensure that national learner entitlements remain, along with statutory duties for the local bodies to provide courses and support for students. The national qualification and inspection frameworks would also be maintained, and would ensure a degree of comparability.

Such a structure should be kept as simple and direct as possible, so the number of intermediary bodies would have to be significantly reduced. As seen earlier, the 47 Local Learning and Skills Councils at the sub-regional level have become redundant, and will be abolished by the Further Education Bill. The Local Partnership Teams, of which there are currently 148, should be made coterminous with local authorities and city regions, and their number is likely to decrease as more city regions are created. Stripped of their planning function, the main purpose of these teams would be to represent the national office at the local level, and to facilitate dialogue and sharing of data.

Finally, the role for the regional level should be firmly circumscribed to that of a forum, to facilitate coordination between adjacent local entities. Indeed, in whatever way the local entities are defined, there will always be a need for collaboration across the borders between administrative units – particularly to ensure easiest access to learners close to the border.

These arrangements would mean changes to the role of the national Learning and Skills Council, which would become more of a funding (rather than planning) body, following the model of the Higher Education Funding Council (HEFCE). Its main functions would be:

- to allocate resources to local areas on the basis of need
- to distribute money to further education providers according to local

arrangements
- to monitor providers' financial and managerial health
- to ensure that the quality of teaching is assessed through the inspectorate
- to monitor access to the national entitlements.

This would mean that the resources would flow directly from the national LSC to the learning providers, according to the decisions agreed between the local authorities or city regions and the LSC.

Finally, Sector Skills Councils (SSCs) and Regional Development Agencies (RDAs) should not be allowed to fill in the gap in terms of planning of skills. The role of the RDAs should be to gather information on skills trends and policy from the city regions and local authorities in order to inform their Regional Economic Strategies.

Despite recognising their current shortcomings, the Leitch Review proposes for the SSCs a prominent role, which they seem ill-equipped to perform at present. As was seen in Section 3, giving the SSCs more responsibilities in developing and approving qualifications is unlikely to create qualifications that are any more valuable or recognised than existing ones.

The current role of the SSCs is problematic, and far from being given any additional responsibilities, the SSCs should stop receiving any further state subsidy. Most would disappear. Some might survive if employers found them a useful tool for designing qualifications, collaboration or licences to practice arrangements (such as in the construction sector, for example), but in this case it would be better if they were funded by an employer levy. The resources saved could be used for funding the new flexible entitlement and income-contingent loans for FE students.

Horizontal integration: employment and other educational provision

One of the main advantages of such a simple, devolved structure is that it would facilitate joined-up working in other areas – particularly in employment, initial and higher education, and neighbourhood renewal.

As seen in Chapter 4, more integration is required between Jobcentre Plus and the further education sector in order to ensure continuity of support – particularly for those who are engaged in cycles of unemployment and low-skilled jobs. The DWP and DfES should work more closely together on their respective aims of getting more people into employment and promoting participation and progression in education.

At the local level, the LSC Local Partnership Teams should be given the lead responsibility for overseeing provision delivered within Jobcentre Plus programmes. Collaboration has often been difficult, and the provision commissioned by Jobcentre Plus has not always proved up to standard – particularly in terms of the quality and availability of basic skills training (NEP

2003). In the longer term, the budget for learning provision within Jobcentre Plus should be transferred to the LSC, as has long been suggested.

Local devolution should improve integration with other educational sectors – particularly with school provision. In the longer term, it is likely that the divide between higher and further education will become increasingly blurred. Many HE courses are now offered in further education colleges, and the introduction of tuition fees in HE means that the funding systems have become more similar. It is also possible that tuition fees will lead more students to go to institutions closer to home, thus removing one of the main justifications for undergraduates' preferential financial support system. Although this remains a distant prospect, a merger of the LSC and HEFCE for post-19 provision appears desirable in the longer term.

Finally, the Government currently expects the bulk of personal, community and development learning (PCDL) to be taken over by local authorities, but it has not explained how this transfer should take place. It makes sense for local authorities or city regions to determine the levels of publicly subsidised provision that they want for their local areas. Further devolution of the overall learning provision would ensure that it does not become decoupled from 'first steps' provision offered through PCDL.

Conclusions

There is little evidence that the promotion of market-like mechanisms in the learning and skills sector has brought the expected benefits in terms of quality or even efficiency. Paradoxically, increased planning and regulation seem to have been one of the main consequences of the incorporation of colleges and the introduction of more competition between them. This has moved decision-making away from the ultimate users, and has led to a multiplication of intermediate layers that is costly and inefficient.

The system should be made more responsive to local circumstances, such as the local population characteristics, transport and the demands of its primary customers – both individuals and employers. This requires devolution, both to the frontline providers and to the local democratic government (whether local authorities or city regions).

The agreement reached in London should be replicated across the country. Using a new structure reduced primarily to the local and national levels, the Learning and Skills Council should play the role of a funding body with an enabling and championing function for adult learning, and an expanded role in relation to commissioning of Jobcentre Plus provision. This overview function, together with the national entitlements and inspection framework, should ensure that a degree of quality provision is accessible to all.

6. Conclusions and recommendations

Those who left school at 16 or shortly after with few or no good qualifications to show for their initial education tend to be the individuals who find it most difficult to engage in learning as adults. They associate the classroom with failure and so are less keen to return to it than their peers, and are also less likely to receive training from their employer. Those who are not in work have even fewer chances to participate in learning. This means that those who started their early careers (both in the labour market and in their adult lives) at a disadvantage only see the inequalities gap widen further as they are excluded from opportunities to develop further.

Adult learning has been more of a concern for this government than it has for any previously. New Labour made an early commitment to lifelong learning and significantly increased the amount of resources devoted to further education. However, this stance has not succeeded in putting disadvantaged adult learners on a par with more privileged students, and current budget constraints are likely to hold them back even further.

Significant inequalities remain embedded in the system. Unlike students who do A levels or higher education, adult learners see their choice of provision constrained by government priorities and targets. While A level students can enrol free of charge to study subjects ranging from Ancient Greek to the much-derided media studies, 20-year-olds who have not achieved five A* to C GCSEs will mainly be limited to studying vocational qualifications – usually NVQs. With Train to Gain, even the choice of subject is now increasingly handed over to their employer as well.

The system of entitlements means that those studying towards a level 2 or (for those up to the age of 25) level 3 qualification do not have to pay any fees. This is one important measure brought about by the Labour government. However, an FE student who decides to take some time off work to study full time or part time will find it significantly more difficult to access financial support to meet their living costs than their HE peers. What is more, those studying for a level 3 after the age of 25 are expected to pay the full tuition fees for the course. This is also the case for HE students, but while HE students are allowed to access grants and income-contingent loans at a zero interest rate, FE students are not.

In this light, it is also striking to see the different ways in which the various adult learning sectors have been treated. Despite (or perhaps because of) being away from the spotlight most of the time, the further education sector has gone through a phase of permanent revolution in the past 15 years. Although it would be difficult to distinguish which of the marketisation or planning drives has gained the upper hand, their combined effect has been one of increasing regulation, and a reduction in the autonomy of further education providers.

Strong schools and universities are considered the 'building blocks' of initial and higher education, but colleges are increasingly expected to compete with new providers for short-term funding and contracts that are entirely determined by the Government's priorities – defined as providing skills for the economy.

In the context of current shake-up of the adult learning system, this report has set out to devise a clear, autonomous rationale for adult learning, and to inform the development of a new framework for publicly subsidised provision in England.

Recommendations

The key recommendations from this report are as follows:

- Articulate a new rationale for adult learning
- Put learners and learning at the centre of the system
- Support learner choice
- Enable learning providers and local government to respond to local demand.

Each of these is explained in detail below.

Recommendation 1: Articulate a new rationale for adult learning

A better balance needs to be achieved between the various objectives of adult learning. The new framework should recognise that improving labour market outcomes for individuals, and the wider benefits of learning for individuals, the family and the community, are as important as providing skills for the economy. Crucially, if the macro-economic and fiscal objectives are to be reached, they too need to focus on learners, rather than on the economy. Policy should aim to help create well-rounded individuals who are fully integrated within society and the labour market.

People should be able to learn new skills when they feel the need for them, and should be encouraged to learn in order to move on from unemployment or economic inactivity. Those who are most disadvantaged should be actively sought in order to help them gain confidence and integrate in their communities.

Government subsidy for adult learning needs to focus on priority groups and to make sure that members of these groups can easily access an appropriate range of learning options that provide the employment and social or personal improvement skills they need. Those with no or low qualifications, people who are long-term unemployed and specific categories of economically inactive people, such as returning mothers, need access to increased support. At the same time, the Government needs to ensure that everyone has access to affordable, good quality provision, for which they may need to pay some or most of the cost.

The system should start with the learner. Those who benefit from an entitlement should be given the right to choose what type of provision they want to access, and should receive further support in order to do so. Learning providers and local government should be strengthened and given more autonomy to allow them to respond to learners' demand, as opposed to the demand defined by Sector Skills Councils or central government.

Recommendation 2: Put learners and learning at the centre of the system

Learners should be entitled to make their own decisions about the type of learning they would like to embark upon, and should be able to focus not just on obtaining qualifications, but also on the process of learning and acquiring new skills.

A new flexible entitlement should be devised for those without a level 2 qualification. This would give students the equivalent of two years' full-time study, to be taken flexibly at any point in time. They would be allowed to work towards a level 2 qualification by starting at entry level or level 1. This would enable them to take only partial qualifications – for example, if they only needed to gain a few additional GCSEs in order to complete their level 2. As with the current system, they would still be able to progress directly to level 3 if they were able to jump a level, and the existing entitlements to study towards qualifications – basic skills, first full level 2 (or 3 up to the age of 25) – would remain.

Learners benefiting from an entitlement should also be given the choice to study towards a qualification if they so wish, and to choose that qualification. However, not all courses should be expected to lead to externally accredited qualifications. Colleges should be able to develop their own awards and qualifications in order to respond to the needs of their learners, with a degree of external validation potentially offered by the Open College Network or the Qualifications and Credit Framework. Courses should also be built to provide general education for adults, including at level 2, as an alternative to the almost exclusively vocational qualifications that are currently on offer.

The Train to Gain programme should be modified or scrapped and its resources used to pay for the new flexible entitlement. Indeed, employers should pay for training towards their needs by themselves, to avoid creating an expectation that all such costs should fall back on the state. Most of the employees currently in the programme would continue to be able to access the same provision, under one of the entitlements, the only difference being that they would be able to choose their course and to set their sights on progressing, rather than merely fitting the needs of their current jobs.

Pilots could be launched to test two options – first, the new flexible entitlement, and second, a revised version of Train to Gain in which employees would be able to choose the type of provision on which they would like to enrol.

Flexible entitlements should be supported by an improved system for information, advice and guidance. In-depth guidance, available both by telephone and face to face, should be easily accessible, and it would make sense to rationalise the current system, with learndirect as the sole, nationwide agency.

Recommendation 3: Support learner choice

Learners' choices should be supported with adequate and coherent funding and financial mechanisms. The current move away from blanket fee subsidies and fee remissions on non-priority courses is a justified means of ensuring that existing resources are targeted at those who need them most.

However, the money saved in this way should be redirected towards supporting those who do not have the means to study. Not only those who are entitled to free tuition but also those who have to pay their fees may need additional support for indirect costs of learning, such as transport, childcare, or living expenses. Discretionary funding, as currently offered through colleges' Learner Support Funds and fee remissions, is the best way of helping students pay for indirect and one-off costs.

College and Career Service advisers should be held accountable for allocating funds on the basis of student need, with particular regard to income. For those studying at level 2 and below, they might also offer some support towards living costs, alongside local grant systems.

Adults taking level 3 and 4 courses in the learning and skills sector should be given access to income-contingent loans, on the same basis as HE students. Although the zero interest rate is regressive, it should be extended to FE learners, who tend to be more disadvantaged, in order to give them the same benefits as their HE peers. The Government should then reconsider the issue when it revises the HE funding settlement in 2009.

Practical arrangements are needed to facilitate access to learning for people receiving Jobseeker's Allowance. While they would still have to comply with job-searching requirements, they should be allowed to study full time up to level 3 as long as they are unemployed. This would mean scrapping the 16-hour rule for study. Welfare benefit recipients should also be encouraged to seek information, advice and guidance for career and learning options early on, even if these are self-financed.

In addition, when someone who has been claiming benefits does start work, better coordination between the LSC and Jobcentre Plus would enable them to finish a course that they started when they were unemployed, in their own time. Ultimately, the learning provision responsibilities of Jobcentre Plus should be transferred to the LSC.

Recommendation 4: Enable learning providers and local government to respond to local demand

Ensuring more choice for learners, rather than central planning, would mean that frontline providers and local government would need to be empowered to identify and respond to local demand within the system of national entitlements.

Like universities, further education colleges should be able to play a strategic role, defining their own mission and direction. Three-year plans should be generalised, in order to allow colleges to plan for the mid term and long term. These plans would be agreed with local government and the funding body. Providers would then be held accountable, after the event, for the way in which they spent the money against the plan.

Local government should be recognised as the learning providers' main interlocutor in ascertaining what the demand is for learning, and how best to respond to it. In line with the agreement reached in London, the funding body would be required to spend the budget for any given area according to the priorities and agreements reached by the local government and learning providers. This would be akin to 'dual key' arrangements, giving the national LSC and local government joint control over the post-19 skills budget. In many cases local authorities would remain the main administrative unit, but as and when city regions are created, these should become responsible for learning and skills.

In order to make space for local government, the LSC structure would need to be significantly reduced, with the national office remaining as a funding body, allocating resources to local areas on the basis of need, and monitoring the spending of learning providers. The Local Partnership Teams should be made coterminous with local authorities and city regions, and would see their role limited to representing the national office at the local level. The regional offices would also have a much more restricted role, acting as a forum to facilitate coordination between adjacent local entities.

Meanwhile, Sector Skills Councils and Regional Development Agencies should not be allowed to plan for skills. RDAs should have their role limited to bringing together information on skills trends and policies from their local authorities and city regions, and state subsidy for SSCs should be abolished. Taken together, all these measures could go some way towards creating a leaner and less expensive structure.

Adults who dropped out of their initial education early on and have not managed to gain valuable qualifications as teenagers need to be given the same degree of choices as their more successful, and often more advantaged, peers. The system should be geared towards supporting and empowering them to make these choices. More flexible entitlements, adequate financial support and more devolution to the frontline should be the building blocks of a renewed system. This would allow adults to have a second chance in education, in order to improve their personal, social and labour market perspectives, and to help them make a full contribution to society and the economy.

References

Abramovsky L, Battistin E, Fitzsimons E, Goodman A and Simpson H (2005) *The Impact of the Employer Training Pilots on the Take-up of Training Among Employers and Employees*, research report 694, London: DfES

Aldridge F and Tuckett A (2006a) *Green Shoots? The NIACE survey on adult participation in Learning 2006*, Leicester: NIACE

Aldridge F and Tuckett A (2006b) *In a Quandary. Who should pay for learning?* (Taken from the 2006 NIACE Survey on Adult Participation in Learning), draft report, Leicester: NIACE

ALI/Ofsted (2005) *Centres of Vocational Excellence in Practice. A survey report on 40 CoVEs in five skills sectors*, Coventry: ALI

Ashton C, Oliver-Watts S, Holden-Smith J, Townsley S, Cramman J, Willis S, Davies B, Wallace J and Warriner L (2005) *ALI Employer Training Pilot Survey*, research report 695, London: DfES

Blanden J, Gregg P and Machin S (2005) 'Educational inequality and intergenerational mobility' in Machin S and Vignoles A (eds) *What's the Good of Education? The economics of education in the UK*, Princeton and Oxford: Princeton University Press

Bureaucracy Review Group for Further Education and Training (2004) *Annual Report 2004*, Sheffield: Bureaucracy Review Group

Byrne D and Raffe D (2005) *Establishing a UK 'Home International' Comparative Research Programme for Post-compulsory Learning*, LSRC research report, London: LSDA

Callender C (2006) *Beg, Borrow, Steal or Save. FE students, tuition fees and the new skills strategy*, London: LSDA/CfBT

Centre for Research on the Wider Benefits of Learning (2006) *The Wider Benefits of Learning: A synthesis of findings from the centre for research on the wider benefits of earning 1999–2006*, research brief 2005/06, London: DfES

Challis M and Pye K (2003) *Fees in Colleges: A review of the use of discretionary fee remission in further education*, research report 496, London: DfES

Chitty C (2004) *Education Policy in Britain*, Basingstoke: Palgrave

Confederation of British Industry (CBI) (2006) *Working on the Three Rs: Employers' Priorities for Functional Skills in Maths and English*, London: CBI

Dearden L, McGranahan L and Sianesi B (2004) *An In-Depth Analysis of the An In-Depth Analysis of the Returns to NVQs Level 2*, London: LSE

Delorenzi S, Reed J and Robinson P (eds) (2005) *Maintaining Momentum. Promoting social mobility and life chances from early years to adulthood*, London: Institute for Public Policy Research

Delorenzi S and Robinson P (2005) *Choosing to Learn. Improving participation after compulsory education*, London: Institute for Public Policy Research

Denholm JW and Macleod D (2003) *Prospects for Growth in Further Education. A review of recent literature for the 'Prospects for Growth' project*, London: LSRC

Department for Communities and Local Government (DCLG) (2006a) *Strong and Prosperous Communities*, Local Government White Paper, Cm 6939-I, London: HMC

DCLG (2006b) *The Greater London Authority: The Government's final proposals for additional powers and responsibilities for the Mayor and Assembly*, policy statement, London: DCLG

Department for Education and Employment (DfEE) (1998) *The Learning Age: A renaissance for a new Britain*, Cmnd 3790, London: DfEE

DfEE (1999) *Learning to Succeed: A new framework for post-16 learning*, Cmnd 4392, London: DfEE

DfEE (2000) *Skills for all: Proposals for a National Skills Agenda* Final Report of the National Skills Task Force, London: DfEE

DfEE (2001) *Skills for Life. The national strategy for improving adult literacy and numeracy skills*, London: DfEE

Department for Education and Skills (DfES) (2002) *Success for All. Reforming further education and training. Our vision for the future*, London: DfES

DfES (2003) *The Skills for Life Survey. A national needs and impact survey of literacy, numeracy and ICT skills*, research report 490, London: DfES

DfES (2004) *Five-Year Strategy for Children and Learners*, Cm 6272, London: DfES

DfES (2006a) *Departmental Report 2006*, Cm 6812, London: DfES

DfES (2006b) *Further Education: Raising skills, improving life chances*, Further Education White Paper, Cm 6768, London: DfES

DfES/Department of Trade and Industry (DTI)/HM Treasury (HMT)/Department for Work and Pensions (DWP) (2003) *21st Century Skills. Realising our potential. Individuals, employers, nation*, Cm 5810, London: DfES

DfES/DTI/HMT/DWP (2005) *Skills: Getting on in business, getting on at work*, Skills White Paper, Cm 6483, London: HMG

Department for Work and Pensions (DWP) (2006) *A New Deal for Welfare: Empowering people to work*, Cm 6730, London: DWP

Dewson S, Tyers C, Pollard E, Bates P (2003) *Learner Support Funds Evaluation*, London: DfES

Esping-Andersen G (2005) 'Social inheritance and equal opportunities policies', in Delorenzi S, Reed J and Robinson P (2005) *Maintaining Momentum. Promoting social mobility and life chances from early years to adulthood*, London: Institute for Public Policy Research

Feinstein L (2002a) *Quantitative Estimates of the Social Benefits of Learning, 1: Crime,* 'wider benefits of learning' research report no 5, London: Centre for Research on the Wider Benefits of Learning

Feinstein L (2002b) *Quantitative Estimates of the Social Benefits of Learning, 2: Health (depression and obesity),* 'wider benefits of learning' research report no 6, London: Centre for Research on the Wider Benefits of Learning

Felstead A, Gallie D and Green F (2002) *Work Skills in Britain 1986–2001,* Nottingham: DfES

Fletcher M (2005) *FE Colleges in the Learning and Skills Landscape – Issues around the institutional structure of further education,* unpublished

Fletcher M (2006) *Supporting Adults in FE: Organisation and impact,* presentation at CfBT seminar, 5 September, unpublished

Foster A (2005) *Realising the Potential: A review of the future role of further education colleges,* DfES

Gamble J (2006) *Creating a More Flexible System: The role of the foundation learning tier,* seminar presentation, ippr, London, 28 June, unpublished

Goodman A and Sibieta L (2006) *Public Spending on Education in the UK,* IFS briefing note no 71, prepared for the Education and Skills Select Committee, London: IFS

Gray M, Peters J, Fletcher M and Kirk G (2002) *The Impact of Individual Learning Accounts. A Study of the early and potential impact of ILAs on learning providers and learning,* research report, London: LSDA

Higher Education Funding Council for England (HEFCE) (2006) *Pathways to Higher Education: Access courses,* HEFCE

Hillage J, Loukas G, Newton B and Tamkin P (2006) *Employer Training Pilots: Final evaluation report,* research report 774, London: DfES

Hodgson A, Spours K, Coffield F, Steer R, Finlay I, Edward S and Gregson M (2005) *A New Learning and Skills Landscape? The LSC within the learning and skills sector,* London: TLRP/ESRC

House of Commons Committee of Public Accounts (2006) *Skills for Life: Improving adult literacy and numeracy, 21st report of session 2005/06,* HC 792, London: The Stationery Office

House of Commons Education and Skills Committee (2006) *Further Education. Fourth report of session 2005–06,* HC 649, London: The Stationery Office

IFF (2003) *Study of Learners in Further Education,* research report 469, London: DfES

Jenkins A and Wolf A (2005) 'Employers' selection decisions: the role of qualifications and tests', in Machin S and Vignoles A (eds) *What's the Good of Education? The economics of education in the UK,* Princeton and Oxford: Princeton University Press

Keep E (2006) *Market Failure in Skills, SSDA Catalyst 1*, South Yorkshire: SSDA

Learning and Skills Countil (LSC) (2004) *Investing in Skills: Taking forward the skills strategy*, LSC consultation paper on reforming the funding and planning arrangements for first steps, personal and community development learning for adults, Coventry: LSC

LSC (2005a) *Priorities for Success. Funding for learning and skills 2006–2008*, Coventry: LSC

LSC (2005b) *Learning and Skills – The Agenda for Change*, Coventry: LSC

LSC (2006a) *National Employers Skills Survey 2005: Main report*, Coventry: LSC

LSC (2006b) 'Train to Gain employer training scheme goes national', press release, 13 September, Coventry: LSC

LSC (2006c) *Funding Guidance for Further Education in 2006/07*, Coventry: LSC

Learning and Skills Development Agency (LSDA) (2005) *The Review of the Future Role of FE Colleges and The Hutton review: the potential contribution of the learning and skills sector to the Lisbon agenda*, LSDA comments, London: LSDA

Leitch S (2005) *Skills in the UK: The long-term challenge*, interim report, London: HMC

Leitch S (2006) *Prosperity for All in the Global Economy – World class skills*, final report, London: HMC

Lucas N (2005) *Purpose Role and Mission: The impact of incentives upon college behaviour*, paper for the Foster Review of Further Education, London: DfES

Machin S, McIntosh S, Vignoles A and Viitanen T (2001) *Basic Skills, Soft Skills and Labour Market Outcomes: Secondary analysis of the National Child Development Study*, research report 250, London: DfEE

Macleod D (2005) *Modelling Progress Towards the Level 2 Target*, London: LSDA

Marshall A and Finch D (2006) *City Leadership. Giving city-regions the power to grow*, London: Centre for Cities

McIntosh S (2004) *The Impact of Vocational Qualifications on the Labour Market Outcomes of Low-Achieving School-Leavers*, CEP discussion paper no 621, London: Centre for Economic Performance, LSE

Meadows P and Metcalf H (2005) *Evaluation of the Impact of Skills for Life Learning: Report on sweep 2*, research report 701, London: DfES

Metcalf H and Meadows P (2004) *Evaluation of the Impact of Basic Skills Learning: Report on wave 1*, London: DfES

Michaelson J, Finch S and Pound E (2005) *A Summary of the Evaluation Evidence on the Adult Learning Grant*, RW36, London: DfES

MORI Social Research Institute (2005) *Attitudes to Fees in Further Education*, final report 4, London: DfES/COI

Morrell J, Chowdhury R and Savage B (2004) *Progression from Adult and Community Learning,* research report 546, London: DfES

National Audit Office (2004) *Skills for Life. Improving adult literacy and numeracy, report by the Comptroller and Auditor General,* HC 20 Session 2004/05, London: NAO

National Employment Panel (NEP) (2003) *Welfare to Workforce Development,* report, London: NEP

National Institute of Adult Continuing Education (NIACE) (2005) *Eight in Ten. Adult learners in further education,* report of the Independent Committee of Enquiry invited by NIACE to review the state of adult learning in colleges of further education in England, Leicester: NIACE

National Research and Development Centre (NRDC) (2005) *Embedded Teaching and Learning of Adult Literacy, Numeracy and ESOL,* research summary 24, London: NRDC

OECD (2003) *Beyond Rhetoric: Adult learning policies and practices,* Paris: OECD

OECD (2005a) *Education at a Glance: OECD indicators,* Paris: OECD

OECD (2005b) *Thematic Review on Adult Learning: United States country note,* Paris: OECD

OECD (2005c) *Promoting Adult Learning,* Paris: OECD

Ofsted/ALI (2003) *Literacy, Numeracy and English for Speakers of Other Languages: A survey of current practice in post-16 and adult provision,* HMI 1367, London: Ofsted

Owens J (2001) *Evaluation of Individual Learning Accounts. Early views of customers and providers: England,* research report 294, London: DfES

Owens J (2002) *Individual Learning Accounts – Follow up study,* RBX 01-02, London: DfES

Page R, Newton B, Hunt W, Hawthorn R and Hillage J (forthcoming) *An Evaluation of the Ufi/learndirect Telephone Guidance Trial,* Brighton: Institute for Employment Studies/NICEC

Performance and Innovation Unit (2001) *In Demand. Adult skills in the 21st century,* London: PIU

Perry A (2005) *Mission, Purpose and Specialisation,* paper for Sir Andrew Foster's Review of Further Education, London: DfES

Perry A and Fletcher M (2006) *The Impact of New Fee Policies in Further Education,* research report, London: LSDA

Piatt W and Robinson P (2001) *Opportunity for Whom? Options for funding and structure of post-16 education,* London: Institute for Public Policy Research

Preston J and Feinstein L (2004) *Adult Education and Attitude Change,* 'wider benefits of learning' research report no 11, London: Centre for Research on the Wider Benefits of Learning

Prior G, Hall L and Lloyd L (2006) *Adult Learning Option Baseline Tracker Study*, research report 392, London: DWP

Qualifications and Curriculum Authority (QCA) (2006a) *Draft Principles for Learner Programmes in the Foundation Learning Tier*, London: QCA

QCA (2006b) *The Qualifications and Credit Framework*, London: QCA

Robinson P (2001) *New Labour, New Economy, New Targets?*, working paper, London: Institute for Public Policy Research

Sianesi B (2003) *A Non-Technical Summary of CEE Work and Policy Discussion*, London: IFS/CEE

Speckesser S and Bewley H (2006) *The Longer Term Outcomes of Work-Based Learning for Adults: Evidence from administrative data*, research report 390, London: DWP

Stanton G (2006) *The Further Education White Paper: Choice and competition in adult learning*, seminar presentation, Institute for Public Policy Research, London, 4 October, unpublished

Stuart N (2001) *Career Development Loan Defaults*, RBX11-01, London: DfEE

Tamkin P, Giles L, Campbell M and Hillage J (2004) *Skills Pay: The contribution of skills to business success*, Brighton: Institute for Employment Studies

Tamkin P (2005) *Measuring the Contribution of Skills to Business Performance. A summary for employers*, Brighton: Institute for Employment Studies

Tennant R, Brown R and O'Conor W (2005) *Level 2 Adult Vocational Learning – A qualitative study of motivations, experiences and outcomes*, research report 664, London: DfES

Torrance H, Colley H, Garratt D, Jarvis J, Piper H, Ecclestone K and James D (2005) *The Impact of Different Modes of Assessment on Achievement and Progress in the Learning and Skills Sector*, LSRC research report, London: LSDA

Torrance H and Coultas J (2004) *Do Summative Assessment and Testing Have a Positive or Negative Effect on Post-16 Learners' Motivation for Learning in the Learning and Skills Sector? A review of the research literature on assessment in post-compulsory education in the UK*, LSRC research report, London: Learning and Skills Research Centre

Tuckett A (2005) *The Untidy Curriculum: Adult learners in further education*, paper submitted to the Foster Review of Further Education, London: DfES

Tyers C and Bates P (2005) *Learner Support Funds: Second evaluation*, CN: 6086a, Brighton: Institute of Employment Studies

Wells A (2006) *Basic Skills and Adult Learning Policy, seminar presentation*, Institute for Public Policy Research, London, 25 April, unpublished

Wells C and Murphy K (2001) *Career Development Loans – Survey of successful and unsuccessful applicants*, brief no 281, London: DfEE

West J (2004) *Dreams and Nightmares: The NVQ experience,* CLMS working paper No 45, Leicester: Centre for Labour Market Studies, University of Leicester

Working Group on 14-19 Reform (2004) *14-19 Curriculum and Qualifications Reform,* London: Working Group on 14-19 Reform